STRANGE
and
OBSCURE STORIES
of the
CIVIL WAR

Tim Rowland
Foreword by J. W. Howard, Superintendent (Ret),
Antietam National Battlefield

SKYHORSE PUBLISHING

STRANGE
and
OBSCURE STORIES
of the
CIVIL WAR

Skyhorse Publishing books may be purchased in bulk at special discounts for sales promotion, corporate gifts, fund-raising, or educational purposes. Special editions can also be created to specifications. For details, contact the Special Sales Department, Skyhorse Publishing, 307 West 36th Street, 11th Floor, New York, NY 10018 or info@skyhorsepublishing.com.

Skyhorse® and Skyhorse Publishing® are registered trademarks of Skyhorse Publishing, Inc.®, a Delaware corporation.

www.skyhorsepublishing.com

10 9 8 7 6

Library of Congress Cataloging-in-Publication Data

Rowland, Tim, 1960-
    Strange and obscure stories of the Civil War / Tim Rowland.
        p. cm.
    ISBN 978-1-61608-395-3 (alk. paper)
    1.   United States—History—Civil War, 1861-1865—Anecdotes. 2.   United States—History—Civil War, 1861-1865—Biography—Anecdotes. 3.   United States—History—Civil War, 1861-1865—Campaigns—Anecdotes. 4.   Curiosities   and   wonders—United   States—History—19th   century—Anecdotes.
I. Title.
    E655.R87 2011
    973.7'3—dc23

                                                2011022880

Printed in the United States of America

Contents

Foreword

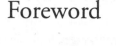

For over fifteen years I served with the National Park Service as the superintendent of Antietam National Battlefield in Sharpsburg, Maryland. I considered this assignment to be a great honor as the battlefield at Sharpsburg is the site of the single bloodiest one-day battle in American history, a place of modern beauty and peace where over 23,000 American soldiers were killed or wounded. This place lends itself to the serious side of war, troop movements, and sacrifice. It cannot be ignored as you look across the beautiful fields surrounding this small Maryland village.

I have learned that this time in American history is often remembered as one of huge movements of blue and gray troops, gallant charges, and victories. Sometimes we forget the individuals who fought these battles, and we think of them as granite statues that dot these cherished sites of American history like Antietam, Gettysburg, and Shiloh. But they are not granite; they were flesh and blood—full of life, laughter, and, on occasion, song. As life was so precious to them they enjoyed what times of peace could be found.

This war, like any other, had its times of irony, times of insanity, and some times of just plain craziness. As long as humans are involved in anything, you will have sorrow and joy and laughter. In the pages that follow you will find the humanity and laughter that were a part of this important time in our history. It is okay to laugh; they did.

—J. W. Howard, superintendent (Ret), Antietam National Battlefield

Acknowledgements

Writing a note of thanks in the Internet era becomes an increasingly abstract task. In previous works I've spent hours in the cramped librarial spaces—kindly but firmly watched by white-haired women who will see no document despoiled under their watch. Research depended on many guiding hands, phone calls, interviews, and friendly tips. Today, it's log on and go. It is no trouble, in literally seconds, to land a gem such as this one, from the diary of Charles Broomhall, 124th Pennsylvania: "South Mountain battle was fought. Sunday. Somewhat cloudy. We were up early. Colonel put (the) Captain under arrest for going into Frederick yesterday taking a number of his men with him and imbibing at the spirit fountain too much."

Broomhall fought in the Cornfield at Antietam; he had failed to hear his commanding officer's order to throw all bedrolls in a pile on the way to the field, which was a good thing because when he unrolled his blankets some time later he discovered his protective blankets had been riddled with thirty-eight bullet holes.

This diary was brought to light by Carolyn Ivanoff of Shelton, Connecticut, a woman to whom I am grateful but have never met. It was disseminated through Antietam on the Web, by a person or people known only to me as "Webmaster."

So I owe a debt to the entire cast of behind-the-scenes scholars, historians, and archivists who have catalogued mountains of material that once upon a time would have been accessible only through long drives and tiring searches of mildewing boxes. Some really incredible information is out there for the picking, and now, even non–classically trained historians such as myself can commit acts of unfettered research that would have been beyond our ken a mere decade ago. Today, we can quote a historian by viewing his YouTube post or see hundreds of old photographs by keywording a Library of Congress search site. Whether this is good or bad, I cannot say. Some elements of the chase have been lost. And so much material is available that deadlines can come and go as one loses himself in thousands of pages of text surrounding the relative meaning of Lee's Lost Orders. It's good stuff, I know, and I was happy to take advantage of these scholarly sites.

But there were times, of course, that I was grateful for the bricks and mortar of a local library or two, such as the one in my backyard at the Hagerstown Community College (HCC). LuAnn Fisher and Karen Giannoumis were always ready and willing to find needed (uncomputerized) material. HCC is also blessed to have on staff Thomas

Clemens, whose knowledge of the war is legend and whose recent work on the writings of soldier-historian Ezra Carman is of incredible value. Tom, his dog Bomber at his feet, was always there when I'd come bursting through his door with embarrassing questions such as, "What's the difference between a caisson and a limber?"

And many have helped along the way, from Tim Johnson who took me on innumerable battlefield tours many years ago (leaving me with the distinct impression that the South had actually won), to Art Callaham, who has recently served as an excellent sounding board. I would also like to thank Sky-horse editor Steve Price, who was always quick and accurate in pointing out what mattered and what didn't, and always awarded me just the right amount of rein.

Finally, this is really the work of two people, even if there is only one name on the cover. My wife Beth was the first reader of each chapter, which is work that might be more closely associated with minesweeping in Third World nations. She discovered and defused many potential problems, and was kind on the occasions that I needed to go back to the drawing board.

Introduction

A decade before video games came on the scene, the Civil War was about all a few of us ten-year-old boys had. Men were going to the moon, it was true, but some of us felt safer putting our trust in things that had actually happened, rather than in books of science fiction filled with unproven events that might one day fail to materialize. So in my circle, we read books by Bruce Catton or Shelby Foote about men named Grant and Lee. The Civil War, baseball, and peanut butter sandwiches were about as good as it got. So why not World War II? Or World War I? Or the Revolutionary War? I don't know. For us, the Civil War resonated, maybe because we Americans were fighting ourselves. That was different.

What I remember of those books by Catton and Company fascinates me to this day. I vividly remember stray fragments of prose: "Lee loved his Texas troops" and Grant arriving on the scene "riding furiously in his mud-spattered pants." But I remember remarkably little of the actual battles that were exhaustively depicted page after jelly-stained page.

Today I understand why that was so. I was fated to grow up to become a journalist with no skill at remembering names and no talent for numbers of any sort. So even back then, when I would read that "Brig. Gen. Elijah Bedliner led the 45th New Jersey against the 15th Mississippi under Maj. Gen. Massentauk Corpussle . . ." the ole peepers would glaze over into casts normally associated with rock candy.

Had I stopped to think about it at the time, I might have surmised that in life I was destined to be a color analyst, seeing that I had no ability at calling the play-by-play.

As a teen, the Civil War succumbed to Space Invaders and was lost to me for many years. I would visit battlefields, it is true, but I kept banging my head into that confounded Brig. Gen. Bedliner and his bloody 45th. I wouldn't go so far as to say that the more I learned about the Civil War the less I understood, but my journey lay somewhere along those lines. My wake-up call came when I realized I could dutifully recite which brigade had done battle with which regiment— but if you had put a Springfield rifle to my head and asked which was bigger, a brigade or a regiment, the jig would have been up.

This book includes plenty of battle scenes to be sure, but they are battle scenes in context of the men, and yes, women, who were behind them, and the strange and often absurd circumstances that contributed to their roles in the fight. It is a book that tips its hat to the fact that very little of what happened in America in the years 1861 to 1865 involved actual battles. There were stupendous conflagrations here and there, but life did go on.

It is also true that I am a humor writer by trade, which might seem counterintuitive for a work such as this. Yet that is the angle I have approached this book from and why it will hopefully contribute a worthwhile, minority perspective in a sea of Civil War literature.

My first fear was that there wouldn't be enough material for a book of Civil War irony and wit; a couple of months into the project, my fear was that there was no room for it all. So many aspects of this war were just so damn strange.

At the U.S. Military Academy at West Point, James Longstreet and Jesse Reno were fast friends. But they fought on opposing sides during the Civil War, and Reno was killed by Longstreet's command at the Battle of South Mountain. Lewis Armistead, meanwhile, was booted from West Point after he brained his nemesis Jubal Early over the head with a supper plate. These two men wound up fighting on the same side.

Early, a man "fluent in profanity," was the heartless fiend who burned residents in several Northern towns out of house and home, yet when a severely wounded Yankee in the Shenandoah Valley complained that the Rebels had stolen his canteen, Early personally got it back, filled it, and allowed the enemy boy to quench his thirst.

It was thirsty Confederate officers in the West who indulged in a little too much Tennessee sippin' whiskey and were too drunk to lead a point-blank attack on a Federal column that slipped by under their noses to the town of Franklin, where a young Confederate soldier wound up leading a charge on his own father's house.

Sitting in his own house during the hostilities of Bull Run, a Virginia man quickly determined that the middle of a battlefield was no place to live life, so he packed up and high-tailed it to a small town in the western part of the state, where the war would never touch him again—a nice little place that went by the name of Appomattox. He wasn't the only one forced out of his home; in Virginia, a relaxing Union army was suddenly deluged by a veritable torrent of wild-eyed rabbits, flushed, it would turn out, by Stonewall Jackson's fast-closing troops.

For sport in between battles, bored soldiers would chase rabbits, both for a good laugh and a good stew. Rabbit stew would be a break from the infamous hardtack biscuits that were so brittle that one soldier reported finding a "soft spot" in one of the crackers. Curious, he pulled the partially masticated biscuit from his mouth and discovered "the soft spot was just a ten penny nail."

Who says the Civil War gods didn't have a sense of humor?

This book is not intended as a work of scholarship; those who wish to learn of regimental troop movements or previously undiscovered battle details will be disappointed. Nor is it a random smattering of trivia suffering a disconnect from anything meaningful. Those seeking "fun facts" will be disappointed as well.

Instead, this book seeks to tell the story of the Civil War in a way that we can easily relate to today—especially if we believe in the maxim that truth is stranger than fiction and that it is frequently the story behind the story that ultimately defines the truth. Included here are sixteen eclectic vignettes (and multiple vignettes within the vignettes), some better known than others, that are intended to expand upon not what we know about the war, but what we think about the war.

This was a war filled with some uproariously funny moments; with men and women getting themselves into impossibly tight spots; with startling coincidences; with moments both terribly bitter and unexpectedly sweet; and with entire courses in history altered by the path of a conical nugget of lead, when the difference of a few inches in one direction or the other might have held sway over generations.

Plenty of facts are known about the war, but these facts also leave no shortage of room for new thought. That was happening, of course, even before war's end.

Despite all the talk of slavery and state rights, for example, a Congressman and a General named Dan Sickles sincerely thought the real cause of the war was whiskey.

A product of Tammany Hall, Sickles knew a thing or two about knocking back the sauce, but even he was impressed by the degree of drunkenness in Congress. There could be no civil debate or compromise, because half of the players were liquored up to the point that they believed they could lick any man in the room. Come to think of it, Sickles might have had a point about the role of whiskey in the war. Similarly, it's hard to read some of the outrageous, fire-breathing prose of newspaper editors North and South and not conclude that they hadn't just returned from a three-Mason-jar lunch. And if there were any sober people stalking the pier in Charleston and shaking their fists at Fort Sumter, they kept their dry rationality well-hidden.

Can a beverage really turn the tide of history? What the South had in terms of sour mash, it was sorely lacking in Folgers. Southern soldiers might capture Federal stores of coffee on occasion and when they did, they would grab for it like an airline passenger would grab for the oxygen mask

xx   Strange and Obscure Stories of the Civil War

in a decompressed cabin. But for the most part they were relegated to engaging in coffeelike experiments, which included roasting and grinding okra seeds. The Union, in contrast, was satisfactorily caffeinated, and it is hard to think that this little extra boost didn't sometimes provide the telling edge. It seems strange to think that a company might repair to the back of the line for a coffee break in the middle of battle, but it happened. The aforementioned Sickles was outraged that a division marching to support him at Gettysburg stopped to boil some coffee before coming to his rescue.

In assembling this work, it's my belief that if we stop to think about how we feel toward people we dislike after we've had a couple of belts, or consider what we personally are like in the morning prior to that first cup of Joe, we might find that we can relate just a little bit more to our ancestors a century and a half back.

It's important to remember too, that one side wasn't fighting people who looked different, talked differently or, really, had hopes, dreams, fears, or values that were materially dissimilar. A family history in Boonsboro, Maryland, tells of two brothers who fought on opposing sides during the Battle of South Mountain. During a break in the action, they clamored down the mountain and ate lunch together before heading back into the fray to once again start shooting at each other. The story can't be proved or disproved, but given the circumstances, it can't be considered outrageous.

When soldiers from the two sides would meet face-to-face in non-battle circumstances, the governing emotion was less hatred than curiosity. Who are these people, and what do they have against us? One small band of Confederates reportedly surrendered just so they could have a closer look at the Yankees' new wonder-weapon, the repeating rifle. For some the war was duty, for some a job. For others the war stirred serious philosophical questions deep in their souls, or became a sport or a game. It began in 1861 with beautiful young ladies waving handkerchiefs at the grinning new recruits as they marched away to battle. Four years later the girls and the lace were gone; green troops moved to the front were sent off only by the hollow stares of hardened, mud-spattered veterans. (But even as the war dragged on, men found ways to soften its edges: veterans would tell new recruits, "What? The quartermaster didn't issue you an umbrella? Don't let him get away with that; go back and demand your umbrella!")

Today, we understand how early enthusiasms for a cause can melt into oily drudgery and discouragement, especially if the opposition proves to be just as doggedly determined as we are. With time, the Southern soldier and writer George Cary Eggleston acknowledged that the war began to look to some like a "ridiculous affair," a war made "upon a catch-word and fought until (we) were hopelessly ruined for the sake of an abstraction." Yet he added this:

> *"Any Northern soldier bred in the South and understanding his duty as a Southerner would have gone to war on the side of the Confederacy just as eagerly as he had served the Union."*

In short, it made sense to them. And the war will make better sense to us if we understand that it was filled with strange incidents . . . just like the strange incidents of today with which we are so familiar, and in truth find so enjoyable. The Civil

War was about battles and troop movements, yes. But it was also about heroism and shortcomings. It was about geniuses and boneheads. It was about what-ifs and might-have-beens. Wrapped in death as it was, more than anything the Civil War was about the idiosyncrasies of life. And so is this book.

CHAPTER 1
John Brown Gets a Visitor

In October of 1859, the abolitionist John Brown made war between the states all but inevitable. It wasn't that his raid upon the Federal arsenal in Harpers Ferry (now West Virginia) had been such an overpowering success. There were so many comedic errors and such bad luck that it almost seemed to be half military engagement, half Monty Python skit.

The plan was, ostensibly, to steal weapons from the government arsenal and then pass them out to slaves who would join in an epic revolt, gathering steam as it rolled to the South. It might have had a better chance of success had anyone bothered to fill the slaves in on the specifics; but either they didn't know of Brown's scheme, or they were not terribly interested in participating in a plot that could get them hanged. Whatever the case, the twenty-one raiders under Brown had to go it alone, and they made poor work of it. The first casualty, killed mistakenly by Brown's own men, was a free black man who worked as a night watchman for the railroad. The last casualty, it might be said, was the Vermont minister who presided over Brown's burial.

John Brown's raid itself was put down in short order by a band of Marines led by none other than Robert E. Lee, but to Southerners, the event smelled of much more than gunpowder. To the South, the message was this: Any man, any neighbor, no matter how trusted or respected, could morph into a wild-eyed loon bent on leading slaves in revolt. After all, before shedding his skin of normalcy and all but growing the horns of Lucifer, Brown had seemed to his new neighbors as unremarkable as a log farmhouse by the side of a dirt road.

Brown had rented such a house the summer before the raid under the name of Isaac Smith, and his accomplices had drifted in over the course of several months to train for the assault, which they did under the cover of night. It didn't matter what part of the country he was in—North, South, East, or West—the sight of black and white men carrying weapons and drilling together in military formation was inevitably going to cause some awkward questions to be asked.

After the raid, however, everyone was asking the same question, and it wasn't awkward, it was obvious: What makes John Brown tick? At least part of the answer could have been found in the heart of the Northern wilderness.

One of the more interesting snapshots we have of Brown— the man, not the fanatic—had been taken a decade prior, and it ranks as one of history's more unlikely coincidences involving two of the greatest abolitionists of the time.

Brown's permanent hideout was an almost comically secluded farm deep in the Adirondack Mountains of New York—near present-day Lake Placid—that he had purchased in 1849. Ski jumpers and bobsledders now pursue their sports in what would have basically been Brown's backyard. At the midpoint of the 1800s, Brown's farm would have been all but unreachable. It was in the heart of a range of 4,000-foot peaks penetrated by only the most primitive of wagon paths. It was here he stayed in between his abolitionist mischief well to the south and west.

His home was also a weigh station and/or terminus on the Underground Railroad, but the land was more than just a safe harbor. It was a project designed to set up former slaves with the resources they needed to make it on their own. In coordination with a landowner named Gerrit Smith, Brown was subdividing property and teaching runaway slaves to farm on their own—it was a case of civil rights meeting sustainable agriculture.

Early critics of the project, however, were not impressed. Adirondack banker-turned-historian Alfred Lee Donaldson said that relocating blacks from Southern saunas to the near-Arctic conditions of the mountains "was about as promising of agricultural results as would be the placing of an Italian lizard on a Norwegian iceberg."

And Donaldson (writing in 1920) was just getting warmed up:

> *The farms allotted to the negroes consisted of forty acres each, but the natural gregariousness of the race tended to defeat the purpose of these individual holdings. The darkies began to build their shanties in one place, instead of on their separate grants. Before long about ten families had huddled their houses together down by the brook. The shanties were square, crudely built of logs, with flat roofs,*

out of which little stovepipes protruded at varying angles. The last touch of pure negroism was a large but dilapidated red flag that floated above the settlement, bearing the half-humorous, half-pathetic legend "Timbuctoo"—a name that was applied to the whole vicinity for several years.

John Brown only adopted the more familiar, hairier visage as a disguise. In earlier years he was more finely coiffed. (Courtesy National Archives)

How a flag could represent "pure negroism" is difficult to say, but Donaldson's account is somewhat emblematic of the indifference, or worse, felt by the natives toward their not-so-favorite son, then and now. Even in 2010, when the state was facing budget shortfalls, the Brown Farm was among the first state shrines to be suggested for cutbacks. More recent scholarship describes the black farming community as more complex than Donaldson's account would have us believe, and attributes it to kindling Brown's respect for black men and women and sharpening his resolve to take concrete action in their interests. Nevertheless, the project was apparently abandoned after only a couple of years, and it was John Brown in a nutshell: Poor results born of pure intentions.

Life wasn't much of a picnic for anyone trying to work the cold, rocky land, including the Browns themselves. The patriarch and elder sons were often away marauding, and his girls would sell berries to raise enough pennies to pay the postage on a letter to their father. On more than one occasion his finances were shored up through the contributions of abolitionists dedicated to his cause. What neighbors there were watched the life and times of the Brown family with some incredulity. For a while, until he sold them to raise funds, he owned a prize-winning herd of Devon cattle, and even a horse, which was a curiosity in the oxen-centric world of the remote northern woods. This was not to mention the black men and women coming and going at all manner of day and night.

Into this surreal racial world stumbled the writer and attorney Richard Henry Dana, best known as the author of *Two Years Before The Mast*, who was vacationing in the Adirondacks in the summer of 1849, when his party became hopelessly lost in the thick forest. After surviving a miserable night with nothing to eat but a four-inch trout divided three ways, the group discovered a path and a piece of property that had the makings of a somewhat plausible farm. "The position was a grand one for a lover of mountain effects; but how good for farming I could not tell," Dana wrote in *Atlantic* magazine twenty years later.

As luck would have it, the farm, or quasi-farm, was John Brown's. As luck would also have it, Dana was a founder of the Free Soil party and an abolitionist—but even he had trouble taking in the scene unfolding before his eyes. After being fed and cared for by Brown's daughter, he witnessed the man himself trundling into view, walking (walking!) before a wagon that was carrying (carrying!) two recently liberated slaves. The runaway-slave couple was also in attendance at the dinner table that night, and Brown solemnly commenced with introductions, referring to everyone, including the erstwhile slaves, by their surnames and the appropriate prefix. This caused some confusion, apparently, as the couple looked around the room to see who this "Mr. Jefferson" and "Mrs. Wait" might be, before realizing that Brown was referring to them. And eating supper at the same table as a white family was almost more than they could stand. "They had all the awkwardness of field hands on a plantation; and what to do, on the introduction, was quite beyond their experience," Dana wrote.

At the time, of course, Brown was just a two-bit agitator, and to Dana the name was meaningless. He was just a simple farmer who had the odd habit of collecting ex-slaves. Dana found Brown to be intelligent, courteous, and a man of dignity, "that dignity which is unconscious, and comes from a superior habit of mind." There was no sign of zealotry, just "a clear-headed, honest-minded man who had spent all his days as a frontier farmer. On conversing with him, we found him well-informed on most subjects, especially in the natural sciences. He had books and evidently made diligent use of them."

That was it. No discussion of slavery, abolition, or politics. There was no mention of the cause both men held dear (perhaps out of manners because there were always blacks present, Dana later speculated), and each man remained ignorant of the other's missions. Dana was off on a journey overseas in 1859–60 when he began to hear bits and pieces of what had transpired in Harpers Ferry at the hands of a man named Brown from North Elba, New York. It didn't take long to put two and two together, but the chance meeting of ten years before was still incredible to contemplate:

> *It would have been past belief had we been told that this quiet frontier farmer, already at or beyond middle life, with no noticeable past, would, within ten years, be the central figure of a great tragic scene, gazed upon with wonder, pity, admiration or execration by half a continent. That this man should be thought to have imperiled the slave empire in America, and added a new danger to the stability of the Union! That his almost undistinguishable name of John Brown should be whispered among four millions of slaves, and sung wherever the English tongue is spoken, and incorporated into an anthem to whose solemn cadences men should march to battle by the tens of thousands! That he should have done something toward changing the face of civilization itself!*

Not everyone with an English tongue was singing Brown's praises, obviously, and the final chapter in Brown's story in the North represents what he was up against, even on his home turf.

Upon his execution in December 1859, in Charles Town, West Virginia, Brown's body was released to his wife and a party that would help transport it by rail back to North Elba—the prophetic Brown had carved his tombstone before heading south. The journey did not go smoothly. Crowds pro and con awaited the small procession at the train depots, and in Philadelphia, the authorities even had to rig up a dummy coffin as a decoy. Slowly, family and friends commenced up the east shore of Lake Champlain, then crossed it by ferry and headed into the deep mountains and woods.

The Rev. Joshua Young was minister of the Unitarian Church in Burlington, Vermont, but less known was his position as an important cog in the Underground Railroad. In a letter to a confidant he wrote, "How many tales of cruelty I listened to, how many backs scarred by the slave driver's lash and some not healed, I looked upon, how many poor scared creatures I secreted in cellars or garrets until the danger was past I cannot tell, only this I did again and again, both while living in Boston and in Burlington."

So Young had an interest in attending the burial of John Brown, although he later indicated that it was not a serious interest and that it was only after being petitioned by a parishioner on the street—a "more ardent" abolitionist than himself—that he agreed to venture to Brown's final resting place.

An ample gathering had assembled at North Elba, but apparently Young was the only minister in attendance, and it was requested of him to conduct the funeral ceremony. "Of course there was but one answer to make to such a request—from that moment I knew why God had sent me there," Young wrote later in life.

If God understood the situation, He failed to inform Young's congregation. This was not a time when news traveled fast, but even so, by the time Young returned home to Burlington, he learned that six of his wealthiest parishioners had quit the church. Several more quit soon afterward. "Friends avoided him upon the streets," wrote Donaldson. "The papers all over the country, with few exceptions, vilified and caricatured him. He was the butt of tongue and pen from coast to coast. He was branded an "anarchist," a "traitor," an "infidel," a "blasphemer . . ."

By Young's own reckoning, he had gone from a respected preacher to a "social outcast" in two days. He refrained from defending himself until well after the fact, despite the pleas of his family. It might be assumed that, at the time, laying low was the more prudent course, since parishioners who were upset with their minister for laying Brown to rest might not be tolerant of the whole Underground Railroad situation.

Young did have his day, finally. When the remains of ten other members of the raiding party were returned to Brown's farm for permanent burial, Young was again present to lead the services—this time to lusty acclaim.

CHAPTER 2
Abner Doubleday Throws the First Pitch of the Civil War

No man may be better known for what he didn't do and less known for what he did than Abner Doubleday. Had he known that he would get credit for inventing the great game of baseball, Doubleday might have been more willing to forget the slight he received at the hands of Gen. George Meade at the battle of Gettysburg and the loss of Fort Sumter.

Doubleday did indeed invent something that everyone has heard of—the famed San Francisco cable car system, although he isn't known for that either. Instead, as word associations go, Doubleday and baseball have become as common as balls and strikes.

It's true that in his idle, youthful hours, Doubleday was known to map out recreational pursuits, although if a four-base diamond was among Doubleday's doodlings, he never mentioned it to anyone or attempted to take credit when the game gained in popularity (and Doubleday was not a man to downplay his accomplishments). Nor was baseball among the credits listed in his obituary in the *New York Times*.

In a sense, though, the Doubleday baseball myth was, at the time, as much a boost to his country as was his war service. At the turn of the century there had been some rumblings that the majestic and purely American sport of baseball was not so American after all, and was merely a warmed-over version of the English game of rounders. This view didn't serve America's sporting icons or, more specifically, its sporting-goods icons well.

So in the early twentieth century, Albert Spalding—a former player and owner and founder of the sporting goods empire—formed a commission to get to the bottom of this baseball thing once and for all. The conclusion was forgone, but some historical back-filling was needed to justify the decision. In the middle of assembling his commission, Spalding received a letter from a man named Albert Graves who claimed that Doubleday, in Graves's presence, had written out the rules for the game in Cooperstown, New York, in 1839.

What this story lacked in documentation it made up for in convenience, since the date would indicate that baseball was born and bred in America. Spalding's commission reported in 1907 that baseball was created just as Albert Graves had described.

"This conclusion was greeted with considerable joy, as it fed Americans' pride and once again established America's independence from Great Britain and such British games as cricket and rounders . . ." wrote sports historian Edward Rielly.

Having died fourteen years prior, Doubleday was not in a position to refute the finding, nor was the Cooperstown Chamber of Commerce likely to throw cold water on the story. That job was left to Robert Henderson, chief librarian of the New York Public Library (and obvious communist and anti–apple pie activist), who surgically shredded the Doubleday myth, aided and abetted by the collection of historical baseball paraphernalia donated to the library in 1946. Included in the collection was an illustration of boys playing baseball in Boston in 1835.

Henderson asserted that baseball had even been played by Washington's men at Valley Forge, and the 1946 collection even referred to a baseball-like sport in a book called—one would hope Spalding's pro-American heirs were sitting down when they read this—"Les Jeux des Jeunes Garsons.[*sic*]"

Mon Dieu.

But even with all the evidence at hand, it's a fair bet that more people today "know" that Doubleday invented baseball than "know" that he fired the first shot of the Civil War on behalf of the North—which he actually did.

Along with a small platoon of Federal troops stationed 600 miles south of the Mason-Dixon Line at the port of Charleston, South Carolina, in the winter of 1860 and spring of 1861, Doubleday would literally and figuratively be on an island. These men (10 percent of whom were musicians) were a rowboat of Yankees in a sea of Southern fire-eaters who were raising troops, stockpiling weapons, and agitating for secession. And drinking heavily. As the city residents grew bolder and more menacing, the Federals withdrew under the cover of night to Fort Sumter, a dismal, prisonesque outcrop of brick and stone in the Charleston harbor.

MAJOR ABNER DOUBLEDAY,
Of Fort Sumter.
Entered according to Act of Congress in the year 1861, by M.B. Brady, in the
Clerk's office of the District Court of the U.S. for the So. District of New-York.

Although soldiers in the Civil War passed the time by playing a form of baseball, the game was not the brainchild of Abner Doubleday. (Courtesy Library of Congress)

Doubleday described it this way: "The fort itself was a deep, dark, damp, gloomy-looking place, enclosed in high walls, where the sunlight rarely penetrated. If we ascended to the parapet, we saw nothing but uncouth State flags, representing palmettos, pelicans, and other strange devices."

His interests at the time, of course, were focused on cannonballs, not baseballs. He watched with rising bile and disdain as the South Carolinians inventoried the former government property on the shore, trying to master the military arts. Of primary concern was that the Union had sabotaged the cannonballs it left behind on shore by painting them with coal tar. In fact, cannonballs that were exposed to the elements were routinely varnished with tar so that they would not rust. However, Doubleday wrote in 1876, "It was immediately reported that before leaving we had taken great pains to tar the balls to render them useless. The problem which puzzled the military savants of Charleston was to determine in what way cannonballs were ruined by tar."

So Doubleday reckoned that a sharp Union response to the "spoiled child" of South Carolina would have nipped the whole war thing in the bud. He generally had kind words for his superior officer at the fort, Major Robert Anderson, although he chafed at the leader's inaction in light of on going South Carolina provocations. Anderson held proslavery views, which dovetailed nicely with the actual slaves that he also held. His wife was from Georgia, and while she stayed loyal to him, his brothers-in-law wound up attacking the fort. This was among the first of many complex and conflicting sentiments affecting the minds of men and women of both sides. Anderson's pro-slavery stance was further fueled by a liberal interpretation of the Bible. At one point, Doubleday reminded his commander that the Bible did not apportion slavery on the basis of color, and consequently Anderson himself might make as suitable a slave as any other man.

This brought the debate to an apparent end, at least for the time being.

The Charleston press (through the course of the war, no one was noisier and rattled more sabers than newspapermen—and no one ran faster for cover when hostilities began than local editors) singled out Doubleday for amusement, labeling him an "abolitionist." At the time, there was no greater insult, and indeed, Doubleday wanted to crush both the institution and the uprising.

The Federal government, however, seemed to be doing its best to look the other way. The troops at Sumter petitioned for a warship to come to their relief; instead, the government sent a passenger steamer, *The Star of the West*, to try to restock the fort's larder. The steamer and its desperately needed provisions got within sight of the fort. But when the Southerners fired a few shots in her direction, the captain turned her around and went home to New York. It galled Doubleday that such an unsophisticated military force as Charleston was putting forward might win for the Federal's want of bread. He wrote his wife Mary in late March:

> *The hostile batteries I think must be trying to frighten us. They keep up a tremendous firing with blank cartridges, balls & shells out to sea, to show us what they can do, I suppose. I have no doubt we could whip all their batteries around us in a fair fight, but then from present appearances we might ultimately have to surrender from hunger.*

In the North, people were watching events play out in the South with mixed emotions. Fernando Wood, the strong-arm mayor of gang-riddled New York City sided with the South, largely because his political machine depended on the cash generated by Southern cotton. Wood penned a memo to his council, suggesting that the Union was doomed, so New York City and its environs might as well consider seceding from upstate New York. He proposed the creation of a city-state to be named Tri-Insula, which would have presumably been like Sparta, but with more violence.

The city's council and playwrights, however, were more sympathetic to the Union's cause. Doubleday was much amused to received playbills from Fort Sumter stage productions acted out in New York and Boston, where the small band of holdouts was portrayed as heroic bastions of national ideals.

Meanwhile, the Rebel noose continued to tighten. It was Doubleday's view that the loudest rabble-rousers in Charleston—not all that much loved, even through the balance of the South, he hinted—figured that Washington did not have the stomach for a fight. By striking against the fort, the fire-eaters believed, the Federal government would see that the South was serious and would agree to Southern independence rather than take up arms.

The fly in this tactical ointment was the inauguration of the newly elected president, Abraham Lincoln. (Doubleday, unlike his fellow officers in the command, was a fan of the new president.) Whatever his various and sundry beliefs regarding slavery and other urgent matters of the day, Lincoln was resolute in his idea that the Union must be preserved at all costs. It was an uncompromising stance, Doubleday believed, that the leaders in Charleston had not entirely bargained upon. But the election of the hated Lincoln steeled their own resolve to secede, so by then—even though there were still efforts at peace—too many wheels had been set in motion to facilitate cooler heads.

By the time South Carolina seceded on December 20, 1860, Anderson had decided secretly to regroup behind the protective walls of Fort Sumter. The Southerners scrambled to occupy the abandoned Federal outposts in and around the Charleston harbor in the days after Christmas, and by January 2, Fort Sumter was all the United States government had left. As it turned out, however, the press clippings advertising the structure as a "fort" had been greatly exaggerated. What walls there were, were crumbling under a never-ending assault of windblown sand. It lacked flanking defenses and, in a couple of spots, parts of the walls had been torn down in anticipation of a rebuilding effort that the engineers had somehow never gotten around to.

But Doubleday was ever the optimist: "Perhaps in one sense it added to our security, for there was no glory to be acquired in capturing a fort which was wide open and defenseless."

The fort, and the Federals' feverish work to shore it up, became something of a tourist attraction for the residents of Charleston, who, wearing their secession cockades, would frequently come calling, although they never offered up any violence.

They hardly needed to, so inept were the nation's efforts to look after its own interests. A group of 150 masons were sent to Sumter to fortify the fort's walls, but no one bothered to check their loyalties prior to their dispatch. As (bad) luck would have it, most favored the South and were not terribly interested in the garrison's predicament.

Worse, even on the eve of the Civil War, the Buchanan Administration (Southern sympathizers abounded in the nation's capital) had continued to blithely send thousands of U.S. muskets to the government of South Carolina, while sending only forty to Fort Sumter. This handful of weapons had no sooner arrived than the Secretary of War telegraphed in the middle of the night, asking for them back.

To add insult, while the fort was being lackadaisically patched and weapons were being denied, the Administration sent an inspector to the fort to ensure than everyone there was doing his job properly, even with no materials and provisions to do it. It was about more than Doubleday could stand.

Nor could he stand silent in the face of growing Northern sentiment to simply say "goodbye and good riddance" to the South. Doubleday heatedly wrote that this was an insult to Northerners who had invested capital in the South, and that it was unconscionable for the United States to write off its magnificent Southern harbors, as well as the mouth of the Mississippi and the Chesapeake Bay. All this, Doubleday said, was "a proposition to commit national suicide."

And while Northerner opinion-drivers were agitating against conflict, their Southern counterparts were agitating for it—or at least for secession, whether it led to war or not. Part of their sales pitch was directed toward poor white dirt farmers in the South, who were promised that with secession and the reopening of the African slave trade would come an abundance of cheap negroes. Thirty dollars a head, tops. Southern leaders, Doubleday said, "Tried to make the poor whites believe that . . . every laboring man would soon be a rich slave owner and cotton planter. To the timid there would be no coercion (to fight). To the ambitious, they spoke of military glory and the formation of a vast slave empire, to include Mexico, Central America and the West Indies."

Doubleday tartly noted after the war that cheap slaves never became a reality—the reopening of the international slave trade would have been bad business for the Commonwealth of Virginia, which had an active slave-breeding trade that would have been crippled by a saturation of the market.

Meanwhile, some of the rich plantation owners who had beaten the drum for independence suddenly went silent, it occurring to them that someone would have to pay for the establishment of this "vast slave empire," and that it just might be them. Some anti-secessionists were emphatic. South Carolina judge J. L. Petigru, who was brought to tears by the thought of a divided Union, remarked that he would not be supporting secession because the state was "too small for a republic and too large for a lunatic asylum." But these and other concerns were drowned by the fire-eaters.

Having surrounded the U.S. garrison and for the most part cut off its supply lines in January, the Rebels could have taken Fort Sumter any time they wanted. The reason they waited made sense: Might as well fix up the fort on the United States' dime and capture it once the improvements had been made.

By April, the South was ready for its initial attack. Brig. Gen. P. G. T. Beauregard—they did things this way in the South—sent word to the fort announcing his plans to attack.

Doubleday was underwhelmed:

> *About 4 A.m. on the 12th, I was awakened by some one groping about my room in the dark and calling out my name. It proved to be Anderson, who came to announce to me that he had just received a dispatch from Beauregard, dated 3.20 A.m., to the effect that he should open fire upon us in an hour [D]etermined not to return the fire until after breakfast, I remained in bed.*

Doubleday credits the "venerable" Edmund Ruffin (who, wrote Winston Groom, despised the Yankees with "a hatred that was almost obscene") with firing the first Southern, and thereby the first, shot of the Civil War. Like Doubleday, Ruffin is better remembered for other things, such as his contributions to agronomy. He introduced scientific soil testing and revitalized Virginia's agricultural economy by sharing a new way to rotate tobacco crops for optimum yield. On hearing of Lee's surrender, Ruffin sat down at his writing desk and declared (multiple times) his "unmitigated hatred" for the Yankees before wrapping himself in a Confederate flag and putting a bullet through his head. In a sense, he might so be remembered as firing the last shot of the Civil War.

Ruffin's cannon shot hit the fort wall in "unpleasant proximity" to Doubleday's right ear. Soon, the fort was being pounded by nineteen batteries, filling the fort with smoke, dust, and debris. Doubleday contemplated the action for a while before going down to the mess for breakfast.

His biggest complaint of the morning, oddly, wasn't about the cannon shot, but about the poor quality of the pork he was forced to eat at his morning meal. Breakfast over, he marched his detachment of men to the casemates to return fire.

> *In aiming the first gun fired against the rebellion I had no feelings of self-reproach, for I fully believed that the contest was inevitable, and was not of our seeking . . . The only alternative was to submit to a powerful oligarchy who were determined to make freedom forever subordinate to slavery.*

Doubleday's shot bounced off the roof housing the opposing battery.

The defense of Fort Sumter was of course pointless, and in truth so was the attack. In all, the whole show had the atmosphere of liquor-fueled, chest-thumping bonfires that college students put on the night before the Big Game. Still, the exercise had its moments. The big guns atop the fort were not employed, as Major Anderson was reluctant to use any weaponry that might inflict casualties on a people that he was still apparently having trouble considering as the enemy. This unused arsenal included "modified guns that might have reached the city of Charleston itself. It seemed to me there was manifest desire to do as little damage as possible," Doubleday wrote. But this didn't stop a wild-eyed Irishman from sneaking up the walls and setting off a few charges on his own.

Doubleday's own men eventually abandoned their casemate, only to be baffled several minutes later when they heard its big gun fire. Returning to the little room that held the weapon, they found several of the aforementioned Baltimore masons doubled over in convulsions of laughter. Not only had they figured out (from watching Doubleday's men) how to fire the gun, the beginners had hit their target dead center.

Much of the fort's inner sanctum was built of wood, and when this was set afire by Rebel artillery Sumter was officially doomed. When flames threatened the magazine, the men shut the heavy copper doors to the powder room and hoped for the best. A cannonball soon dented the lock, and after that neither the flames nor the Federals had access to powder and shot.

The cheering mob back in Charleston was calling for Doubleday's head, the belief being that he was the only "Black Republican" in the fort at the time. However, his general good standing among the town leaders allowed him to save his skin—despite one further act of mischief on his part.

A large hotel on shore was seeing double duty as a troop barracks, so Doubleday used this as license to send a forty-two-pound ball crashing through the length of the struc-ture, sending troops and civilians alike scampering for the exits. An aggrieved officer later asked Doubleday why he did it, and—not in the mood for a drawn-out explanation—Doubleday stated that the innkeeper had given him a rotten room three years earlier, and he saw this as his one and only chance to get even. At hearing this explanation of lost honor restored, the Southern officer's face brightened and he fully sanctioned Doubleday's action.

The secessionists' bombardment of the fort did plenty of structural damage, but caused only one serious injury. There were no casualties immediately reported on the Southern side ("Thank God for that," the Union's Anderson reportedly said), making the fight remarkably bloodless—which of course was in contrast to what was to come over the next four years.

The Federals had no option but to surrender the fort after a day of performing admirably in its defense. They were allowed safe passage and the right to salute their flag one last time with gunfire. The salute turned out to be bloodier than the battle. A smoking ember inside the gun caused an explosion when it was packed with powder, killing a soldier by the name of Daniel Hough, who became the first of 360,000 Northern-ers to die in the war. But the cartoonish sideshow didn't stop there. Sparks drizzled out the muzzle of the cannon, setting off a stack of cartridges and blowing several men into the air. They were seriously hurt, but recovered.

The sixty soldiers who defended the fort were treated to two celebrations, one from the Southerners, who threw an aquatic party with all manner of watercrafts to commemorate their victory. The second celebration occurred when the men returned to New York, where they received a hero's welcome, despite the circumstances. "It was impossible for us to venture into the main streets without being ridden on the shoulders of men and torn to pieces by handshaking," Doubleday wrote.

Doubleday would go on to greater achievements, performing well in Gettysburg and the battles leading up to it. Gettysburg might be called Doubleday's finest hour, as his corps of 9,500 men ferociously held off a Confederate force of 16,000 early in the fight. Double received no credit for this either, due mainly to another corps commander who used Doubleday as a scapegoat for his own failures. Maj. Gen. George Meade, never a fan of Doubleday, willingly believed the lie and passed over Doubleday for a deserved promotion. Doubleday left for Washington in a snit.

Although Doubleday's name litters the pages of Civil War history through 1863, little of it has stuck. Other names, even those of men with fewer battlefield accomplishments, have become familiar parts of the Civil War lexicon, but we seldom hear about the man who "invented" baseball. From his writings, Doubleday comes across as a man of humor; there is every chance he would have enjoyed the joke.

CHAPTER 3

Happiness is Throwing Senators in Jail

In Thomas Scharf's *History of Western Maryland, Vol. I,* he notes the following dispatch from aide-de-camp R. Morris Copeland to Maj. Gen. Nataniel Banks, dated Sept. 17, 1861:

> *To Maj.-Gen N.P. Banks:*
> *It is now 5 p.m. We have arrested 12 of the worst men and are progressing very well. We shall get the whole 18 I think, and if any come in on the train to-night we will bag them too . . .*
> *Respectfully,*
> *RMC*

And who were these eighteen lawless men who were being hunted down like dogs in mid-September, 1861? Desperadoes? Thugs? Common bandits? Perhaps. But more to the point of the matter, they were members of the Maryland legislature.

Morris got to live the dream, in a manner of speaking, by taking elected lawmakers into custody, and seemed to enjoy the task as much as many of us would today. Needless to say he had some powerful friends. Abraham Lincoln himself was seeing to it that these duly and legally elected members of the General Assembly were not only deprived of office, but thrown behind bars, where, as far as the president of the United States was concerned, they could rot.

The new president had earlier quipped that he would like to have the Lord on his side, but that he had to have Kentucky. He needed Maryland more. With Virginia and Maryland in the Confederacy, Washington would have been surrounded and the Union would have been in a terribly precarious place before the war had even begun. The South was drooling at the thought of controlling not only the nation's capital, but the strategically crucial Chesapeake Bay as well. So Lincoln was not about to give Maryland's pro-South lawmakers a chance to vote in favor of leaving the Union, especially after his own army had failed so miserably two months earlier at First Bull Run. Things were not good.

How, even Lincoln might have wondered as he ordered the arrests, did we ever get here? The answer was embedded in events of the past nine months, and beyond.

By the dawn of 1861, the idea of secession was not new, nor was it confined to the South, nor was it particularly frowned upon through vast reaches of the young nation.

America's Constitution, at that point, was just three years older than the Soviet Union was when it crumbled. Historically speaking, there was not a lot of time under its belt. In 1861, Gen. Winfield Scott had served under all but two of the country's presidents. As nations go, we might have been seen as a teenager, with all the typical wisdom and restraint inherent in the breed. It would have been no particular skin off many sets of antebellum teeth had Franklin's republic, as he had hinted seventy years prior, proved impossible to keep.

More than ten years before the war, many Southern governors were itching for an excuse to bolt from the Union. They carefully eyed lands to the south, seeing the potential of Mexico and Latin America as great partners in commercial and agricultural enterprises built on the backs of slaves. Land was a way for the South to counterbalance the North's growing industrialism. It was not lost on the South that it produced raw materials, particularly cotton, but that the North performed all the value-added tasks of milling and sewing. Some were figuring out that the South just might have to build its own factories and jettison its Northern brethren altogether, since they always seemed intent on spoiling the Southerners' fun. This would not have bothered more than a few influential Northerners, who viewed the South as a grande dame might have seen a particularly ill-mannered son-in-law.

It was in between these two sentiments that Maryland found herself in the spring of 1861, as Union soldiers were being run out of Fort Sumter and Lincoln was calling for the new conscripts that would soon be run out of Northern Virginia. Maryland's thoughts on secession were divided and complex, and as was true elsewhere throughout the nation, the noisiest factions were not necessarily the most representative. Newspaper editors and fear-mongering lawmakers on both sides breathed fire not universally felt by average people attending to their daily life, who, often as not, just wanted to be left alone. In Baltimore, well-heeled secessionists and state lawmakers agitated for siding with the South; the South wanted to believe that these bellowing voices spoke for the public at large, a leap of faith that was to lead to disappointment. But its hopes were understandable.

Confederate states pulled out all the stops in their courtship. Down on one knee, Virginia called up to Maryland on the balcony, wooing her with stories of their mutual traditions and vision and heaping praise on her noble citizens and leaders. Other Southern states sent envoys to Baltimore, lobbying for Maryland's secession. When candy and flowers didn't work, the South turned to taunts and abuse. To stay in the Union, an Alabama commissioner said, was to "accept inferiority" and become an impotent tool of Union arrogance.

Following the election of Lincoln, Maryland lawmakers had petitioned Gov. Thomas Hicks to call a special session in which the state would go throw her lot in with the South. Hicks was a slaveholder and by all standards a Southerner through and through, but he would not see the Union disintegrate under his watch. That winter and spring he refused to give lawmakers a chance to replicate the choices of lawmakers throughout the South. (For his allegiance, Hicks would later be offered a generalship in the war, but he declined and enlisted as a private for the plausible reason that he didn't know anything about the military; this detail did not deter most men in similar circumstances.)

Even so, Maryland's allegiance at this point was very much up in the air, and the South continued to hold out hope, cheered on by the first fatal clash of the war, in which some residents of Baltimore indeed rose up against "Northern aggression."

The term "wrong side of the tracks" pertained to the region of the community that was downwind of the locomotives' house-blackening and lung-choking smoke. Baltimore at the time solved the problem by prohibiting engines downtown altogether, and the city's northern train station was ten blocks from the road that headed south. Cars had to be pulled from station to station by horse, leaving travelers headed from, say, Philadelphia to Washington, vulnerable to angry mobs. A regiment from Massachusetts was taking this route on April 19, when a throng of brick-throwing Southern sympathizers blocked their path. Citizens, troops, and police ended up in a brawl that left four soldiers and twelve civilians dead.

The action enraged Baltimore native James Ryder Randall, who lost a friend in the hostilities, but, being a New Orleans poet (and not a good one, even by most poets' standards) and professor of literature, didn't have much going for him in the way of talents in the military arts. His small but lasting contribution to the era came about when, in a fit of pique, he penned a lengthy poem imploring Maryland to join the Southern cause.

His work has the tone of a jockey whipping a particularly reluctant nag for all he's worth, complaining mildly that Maryland "wast ever bravely meek," and "thy dalliance does thee wrong," but voicing hope that she will realize that "Better the blade, the shot, the bowl/Than crucifixion of the soul." Taking heart in the Baltimore riots, he proceeds to call Lincoln some nasty names and in celebration of Baltimore's riots, happily concludes "Huzza! She spurns the Northern scum!"[1]

A Maryland glee club with Southern sympathies had set the words—which had been printed in a New Orleans paper—to the tune of "O Tannenbaum" and stood around

---

[1] Somehow, this angry, traitorous work wound up as Maryland's state song in 1939.

the piano sweetly singing of "Howard's warlike thrust." State theory holds that some eighty years after the war, no one much remembered the lyrics beyond "Maryland, My Maryland," and today most state residents are shocked to read the seamy underbelly of their state song. Every so often the Maryland General Assembly tries to change the state song to one that's a little less scumlike, but the effort always comes to naught. The revenge of the jailed legislators, perhaps.

James Randall wasn't the only person inspired by the Baltimore riots. Civil War soldier-turned-historian Ezra Carman, in a work recently edited by Thomas G. Clemens, noted that the *Richmond Examiner* was equally jubilant:

> *The glorious conduct of Maryland decides the contest at hand. With a generous bravery worthy of her ancient renown, she has thrown herself into the pathway of the enemy, and made of her body a shield for the South. The heart of all Maryland responds to the action of Baltimore, and that nursery of fine regiments, rather than becoming the camping ground of the enemy, preparing to rush on the South, will speedily become the camping ground of the South, preparing to cross the line of Mason and Dixon. It is impossible to estimate the moral effect of the action of Maryland.*

The paper simply, and correctly, as it turned out, concluded that the South had no chance without Maryland on its side. It was essential to have "Her territory, her waters, her slaves, her people, her soldiers, her ship builders, her machinists, her wealth, enterprise and bravery."

What the *Richmond Examiner* and many others with Southern sympathies didn't know was that the relative handful of rioters spoke for themselves, not the state as a whole. Indeed, the South's hearty commendations of the riots served as applause the bravely meek state didn't want.

All this left the state government in a tight spot. It did not want to appear sympathetic to the North by allowing Federal troops to pass through its territory to Washington, but it was not ready to leave the Union. If anything, it wished it could be the Switzerland of the Mid-Atlantic.

No one could say for sure where Maryland stood. It was home to nearly 120,000 slaves but had strong populations of European descent whose religions and cultures had no use for the institution. Maryland's past was tied to the South, true enough, but its economy was increasingly of the industrial North. Many of Maryland's elected representatives were for secession, but the people they represented were not.

Maryland wanted states to its north and south to just settle down, even as its own citizens were taking up weapons and lambasting Northern tyrants or Southern traitors, as the case might be. Maryland, while trying to hold up under tremendous pressure from both sides, was in a standoff with Maryland. Some in the Mid-Atlantic states were ready to declare a pox on both their houses and agitate for a "middle confederacy" that would have left New England abolitionists and the cotton states of the Deep South to stew in their own juices, while a great alliance of reason stretching from coast to coast would be a buffer between the two. But at this point, events were moving too fast for any sort of third rail to keep up.

Pro-South lawmakers continued to demand that they be called into session, and Hicks finally agreed to do so in the spring of 1861, after wisely moving the seat of government from Baltimore (on the theory that it was too volatile) to the strongly pro-Union western town of Frederick. Hicks' strategy worked. Having gotten their wish, fire-eating lawmakers couldn't get the body as a whole to pull the trigger. Bills drawn up calling for secession failed to win a majority.

The legislature as a whole, of course, had an inkling that the majority of the people were not on its side. On June 22, the legislature asked the governor to require all local militias to return weapons they had been issued from state armories. In rural Maryland, this demand that people give up their guns went over about as well then as it would today. Home guards passed their own resolutions literally telling the legislature that it could have their guns when it pried them from their cold dead hands.

Seeing the handwriting on the wall, perhaps, Southern sympathizers grew desperate. All manner of rumors, plots, and intrigue supplied tavern-goers with plenty to talk about. Maybe there would be a commando raid on Washington. Maybe some goons could be talked into kidnapping Hicks and dragging him back to Virginia, allowing Maryland's lawmakers free to vote themselves out of the Union without undue gubernatorial influence. In the end, the South didn't act fast enough and the North was not about to take any chances.

In April, Lincoln had written to Gen. Scott, expressing deep reservations about the legalities and the productivity of arresting lawmakers—they had the right to assemble, and further, there was no certainty that this whimsical brood would do the wrong thing. But by the end of the summer, and after the disaster of Bull Run, the luxury of wait-and-see tactics could no longer be afforded. Gen. Stonewall Jackson, for one, was itching to invade Maryland. Across the state, Union authorities got their marching orders. On September 13, Pinkerton detectives arrested a handful of problematic residents of Baltimore and sent them by carriage to Fort McHenry.

As Maryland bickered back and forth over whether or not to se-cede, Gen. Thomas Jackson, sporting the freshly minted nickname "Stonewall," and shown here as a young man, was out of patience and ready to invade. (Courtesy National Archives)

In a colorful letter to Secretary of State Seward, Baltimore attorney Worthington G. Snethen congratulated the government on its action and urged the Union to do whatever it might take to prevent the Maryland legislature, which could not be trusted, from convening. He explained that some pro-Union lawmakers might show up anyway, just to collect the four-dollar-a-day salary. The rest of his derision was directed toward the pro-South newspaper editors in Baltimore, whose arrest caused him "intense satisfaction" and "infinite pleasure." In the end, the Union's martial action in the city, Snethen believed, would be enough to get those disposed toward neutrality off the fence: "The effect of these arrests must determine very rapidly the status of the floating population who are ever on the watch for the stronger side."

Southern sympathizers had been correct; the riots of Baltimore had been a turning point, but not in the manner the South had hoped. Instead, they provided the desperate times that kindled the North's desperate measures. Pro-South lawmakers in Frederick noticed that the roads out of town were suddenly bristling with armed sentries. On September 17, a year to the day before the horrible Battle of Antietam, the rogue elements of the Maryland legislature who remained in Frederick were snapped up and jailed, ending any chance of secession.

"Allow me to congratulate you," Dr. Arthur Rich of Baltimore wrote Seward, "upon the government manifesting its strong arm in giving the quietus to our so-called Legislature. It has soothed down the temper of the disunionists prodigiously."

What they couldn't do through politics, of course, secessionists hoped to do with arms. A year after the legislative cleansing, Lee was crossing the Potomac River into Maryland with hopes that the general public would consider him a great liberator. His officers in Frederick gave rousing stump speeches encouraging men of the town to join the ranks of the South. At last, they said, here was a chance for Marylanders to avenge the bloodshed of Baltimore and the tyrannical treatment of its elected lawmakers.

A few joined up, but not many. For one thing, Lee's own army—disheveled, shoeless, and half-starving—made a poor recruiting poster. Second, money talked, and all Lee could offer local merchants in payment was highly suspect Confederate scrip. But finally, it was the cumulative opinion of Maryland residents that had the final say. Sympathetic as some might have been for the Southern cause, their hearts, and hence their state, never left the Union.

CHAPTER 4

Looks Could Be Deceiving

A wounded Dutchman lay writhing in a makeshift Washington, D.C., hospital following the Battle of Bull Run, a mission that, for the Union, had begun with frivolity and ended in bloody tatters. If the bullets had been brutal on the flesh, the hospital menu wasn't much better in the way of promoting healing. Hard bread, greasy pork, and bitter coffee did not have the same medicinal qualities of chicken soup.

The Dutchman firmly believed his life depended on getting a bite of the fish to which his stomach had been accustomed all his life. He grabbed a young nurse who was making the hurried rounds. "Zee feesh I must have," he implored, as he broke down in tears. "Oh mine Gott, I must have some feesh." Nurses in the Civil War provided both a physical and psychological backbone for the soldiers. They knew what mattered, and this particular nurse, at the first opportunity, scampered to Hunter's Creek, baited a hook, and in a matter of minutes had pulled in . . . a very large eel. No matter, the Dutchman was overjoyed at his special supper and rested well that evening.

He may or may not have thought it odd that the nurse who cared for him was in fact a young man named Frank Thompson who seemed to pay particular attention to comforts that most male attendants might have overlooked. He might have had even more trouble digesting his eel had he known that this man who did the job of a woman was not a man at all, but a woman who would later disguise herself as . . . a woman.

Sarah Emma Edmonds was a complicated girl.

Edmonds decided early on that it would not do to "stay at home and weep," so she cut her hair and enlisted in the 2nd Michigan Infantry. Her upbringing had prepared her for this day. She was born in Nova Scotia, and her father was profoundly disappointed that Sarah was not a boy, a fact that he constantly reminded her of with his fists. Escaping her father was a matter of slipping across the border, dressing as a man, and entering the male-dominated workforce. By the time the war came along, cross-dressing was a piece of cake. (It was also a petticoat that cut two ways; while some women were cross-dressing to get into the army, it was rumored that some men were cross-dressing to get out.)

Edmonds was one of perhaps 500 to 1,000 women on both sides who disguised themselves as men and joined the ranks—dropping one's pants was not a part of army entrance exams in a war that needed every warm body it could get. Any potential soldier who wasn't obviously club-footed and had a reasonable understanding of which end of the rifle to point at the enemy was considered to be good enough.

Nor were there many other obstacles to fitting in with an army of men, curiously enough. A woman might not have fired a weapon before, but neither had a large number of the men prior to service. They all learned as one.

Boys, or virtual boys, were no strangers to the military ranks, so facial hair—or lack thereof—was not an issue. Baggy and bulky wool uniforms concealed a soldier's figure while being amenable to areas of strategic padding and binding, as the need might be. Writing for the National Archives, DeAnne Blanton noted that "Victorian men, by and large, were modest by today's standards. Soldiers slept in their clothes, bathed in their underwear, and went as long as six weeks without changing their underclothes. Many refused to use the odorous and disgusting long, open-trenched latrines of camp. Thus, a woman soldier would not call undue attention to herself if she acted modestly, trekked to the woods to answer the call of nature and attend to other personal matters, or left camp before dawn to privately bathe in a nearby stream."

At least one wife fought alongside her husband and one sister alongside her brother. A woman was shot in the chest at Antietam, and a woman killed at Gettysburg was believed to have participated in Pickett's Charge. Mollie Bean of North Carolina probably fought at Gettysburg too. She served for two years, and when discovered it was assumed that she was a prostitute, which would have been understandable, but when it turned out she wasn't they threw her in the insane asylum. Cathay Williams simply swapped first and last names, and "William" wasn't discovered until (s)he fell sick. In addition to the more obvious trouble a woman might have enlisting in the army, Cathay Williams was black.

Many weren't discovered until they were captured or shot or . . . well, there is the unglamorous story of a couple of women serving surreptitiously under Phil Sheridan who got drunk and fell into a creek. Their rescuers hauled them up to headquarters, where their particular brand of femininity was enough to make even the notoriously coarse general wince. In his memoirs, the only term that came to his mind for one of them was a "she dragoon."

Yet as far as military service was concerned, female fighting wasn't just for the butch. Far from it, really. Mostly they mirrored the men they fought alongside, who were interested in the cause, or even simply the pay. Edmonds, who repeatedly mentions "patriotism," might have been the norm.

If so, that's where her similarity to the rest of the flock, male or female ends. Edmonds was an elegant writer with a dry wit and a good ear for dialect whose book *Nurse and Spy in the Union Army* was a sensation after the war and remains interesting as a tale of the war from a woman's perspective— unlike some men, perhaps, she found it amusing when a local preacher handed out copies of the New Testament with the scribbled advice inside to 1. Put your trust in God, and 2. Keep your powder dry. On arriving in Washington, she also found it curious that "The Capitol and White House were common places of resort for soldiers. Arms were stacked in the rotunda of the one and the lobbies while our 'noble boys in blue' lounged in the cushioned seats of members of Congress, or reclined in easy chairs in the President's Mansion."

In a harbinger of what was to come, the nurse described in detail the rows of hospital tents and the severe need for supplies to tend to the rows on rows of cots filled with disabled men. And this was before the outbreak of hostilities; the swamps of Washington were fine breeding grounds for typhoid, malaria, and other diseases and throughout the course of the war, illness would kill far more men than would bullets.

When the time for the war's first battle (First Bull Run) drew near, the atmosphere was much like the preliminaries to a modern sporting event, Edmonds reported:

> *Oh, what excitement and enthusiasm that order pro-*
> *duced—nothing could be heard but the wild cheering of*
> *the men, as regiment after regiment received their orders.*
> *The possibility of a defeat never seemed to enter the mind*
> *of any. No gloomy forebodings seemed to damp the spirits of*
> *the men, for a moment, but 'On to Richmond,' was echoed*
> *and re-echoed, as that vast army moved rapidly over the*
> *country.*

The attitude began to change the further the army marched into enemy territory. From her (his) position near the rear, Edmonds (Thompson) would hear a volley of rifle fire up front and suspect the battle had been joined. It would usually turn out, however, that the increasingly skittish advance guard had heard a rustling in a hedgerow and unleashed a maelstrom of fiery hell at a pheasant.

Bull Run, or Manassas (which was how Southerners re-ferred to Bull Run), drew the line between talk of blood and blood itself. The difference stunned many. Bragging of mili-tary glory was one thing; listening to the night-long screams of an incoherent, legless soldier driven out of his mind by the pain was quite another. The optimistic hoots and hollers that preceded the battle soon were all gone. Those Federals who were physically able, Edmonds noted, straggled back to Washington and got around to the business of self-medicating: "Every bar-room and groggery seemed filled to overflowing with officers and men, and military discipline was nearly, or quite, forgotten for a time in the army of the Potomac. While Washington was in this chaotic condition, the rebel flag was floating over Munson's Hill, in plain sight of the Federal Capital."

Early on, residents of Washington could have seen Confederate soldiers lounging on Munson's Hill across the Potomac River in Virginia—a vivid reminder of why Maryland had to stay in the Union at all costs. In this sketch of Munson's Hill, a log is made to look like the barrel of a cannon in order to deceive the Yankees into thinking the site is more heavily fortified than it is. These log cannons were known as "Quaker Guns." (Courtesy Library of Congress)

Union Gen. George McClellan's storied hesitancy to take action had one side benefit—by the time he eventually rousted the men to battle, they had all but forgotten that last beating they had been handed by the South. "On to Richmond!" once more resounded through the camp as the troops floated downstream to southern Virginia in the spring of 1862 to engage in the ill-fated Peninsula campaign. Edmonds performed as a nurse and general errand boy, scouting the countryside for food. This chore brought her into close contact with members of her own sex who left her clearly shaken. If Southern men were calling for blood, Southern women, Edmonds felt, had them beat: "The bitter and ferocious spirit of thousands of rebel women in Kentucky, Tennessee, and other States, is scarcely, if at all, surpassed by the female monsters that shrieked and howled for victims in the French Revolution." Her opinion of Confederate men was not much higher, although she allowed that "perhaps prejudice had something to do in making the rebels appear so much inferior to our men."

The slaves liberated by the approaching Federal army were more generous, Edmonds reported: "One old man, evidently their leader, stood up and said: 'I tell you, my breddern, dat de good Lord has borne wid dis yere slav'ry long time wid great patience. But now he can't bore it no longer, no how; and he has said to de people ob de North—go and tell de slaveholders to let de people go, dat dey may sarve me.'"

And there were oddly poignant moments that could only be experienced by a person who was not at liberty to reveal her true identity. Edmonds recognized a friend and fellow Canadian she identified as "Lieutenant V.," with whom she struck up an independent friendship, of sorts, until he was shot to death on the Federal's picket line.

At times my position became very embarrassing, for I was obliged to listen to a recapitulation of my own former conversations and correspondence with him, which made me feel very much like an eavesdropper. He had neither wife, mother nor sister, and, like myself, was a wanderer from his native land. There was a strong bond of sympathy existing between us, for we both believed that duty called us there, and were willing to lay down even life itself, if need be, in this glorious cause. Now he was gone, and I was left alone with a deeper sorrow in my heart than I had ever known before.

Since her enlistment, Edmunds had been angling for a job in espionage, which would have seemed appropriate for a woman of her talents. When a position came open, she went through a lengthy interview process, where "a committee of military stars" with great attention to detail checked her record, patriotism, motives, allegiance, weapons proficiency, and overall character—but happily, not her gender. Then, of course, came the oath. "This was the third time that I had taken the oath of allegiance to the United States, and I began to think, as many of our soldiers do, that profanity had become a military necessity."

Edmonds had "three days to prepare for my debut into Rebeldom," which she was to enter in the guise of a slave. She was able to color her skin readily enough with chemicals but had to wait three days on a wig. Returning to camp in costume, Edmonds was gratified to find no one noticed her, but a bit aggrieved at how few friends an escaped slave, or "contraband," might find among the white race—even among the Northerners. To giver her disguise the ultimate test, she went back to her old boss and asked for work and was sent to the kitchen to make biscuits.

Soon after, Edmonds snuck past the Yankee and Rebel pickets and fell in with a group of slaves taking coffee and corn bread to the troops. Not knowing what to do next, her hesitation drew the attention of a Confederate officer who inquired after Edmonds's master. "I answered in my best negro dialect: 'I dusn't belong to nobody, Massa, I'se free and allers was; I'se gwyne to Richmond to work.' But that availed me nothing, for turning to a man who was dressed in citizen's clothes and who seemed to be in charge of the colored department, he said: 'Take that black rascal and set him to work, and if he don't work well tie him up and give him twenty lashes, just to impress upon his mind that there's no free niggers here while there's a d—d Yankee left in Virginia.'"

Sara Edmonds concluded that it would not do to "sit at home and weep," so the disguised herself as a man and made a major contribution to the Union effort. (Courtesy Michigan State Archives)

The work involved the construction of earthworks, which was difficult enough for the strongest of the men, and, after one day's labor, left her hands in no condition to work the following morning. So she found a negro boy whose job was to carry water to the troops and swapped places with him. To repay the favor, she passed him $5 in greenbacks, but found it shoved back in her face: It was more money than he had ever dreamed of, and he was afraid such a magnificent sum might ruin his life.

Edmonds gained considerable intelligence on the foray, learning the size of the Confederates' army, the number of cannons in its possession, and its upcoming plans—unlike in the Union, Confederate foot soldiers were told of the army's next move in advance. Although she was never discovered, there were several close calls. She needed to behave, because a whipping would have exposed the white skin of her back. And at one point, she was chatting with some slaves when she noticed the eyes of one of her compatriots growing noticeably wider by the second. Finally he elbowed his neighbor and stammered, "Jim, I'll be darned if that feller ain't turnin' white." Sure enough, the nitrate of silver was wearing off. Edmonds told the members of the group that it was to be expected, as his mother was white—and then while they were thinking that one over, she scooted out to reapply the chemical solution.

One particular piece of her gathered information was useful from both a professional a personal standpoint. As she was refilling the soldiers' canteens with water, she saw a peddler approach who she recognized from his visits to the Federal camp, where he sold newspapers and stationery, and usually found an excuse to hang around for a half a day or so. She listened, stunned, as the paper salesman began to spill all manner of Union secrets.

Only one detail seemed to bother his conscious a bit, that being that he had given away the position of "Lieutenant V," a "fine man" who had been killed as a result of his intelligence. Edmonds fought back a cold chill, taking comfort only in the knowledge that from that point on the salesman was a dead man walking.

Meantime, after doggedly driving back the Confederates from the lower James River in a series of relatively successful but costly battles, McClellan's army was now pointed directly at Richmond. Blessed with such an advantageous position, McClellan took immediate action by wiring Washington to complain about how badly outnumbered he was, how greatly the odds were stacked against him unless he received more troops, and how he planned to attack—at some point pretty soon, any time now probably—but he could not be held responsible for a loss, seeing as how the South held every card in the deck. An exasperated Lincoln finally wrote back telling him to attack Richmond or forget the whole thing and come home.

Edmonds, meanwhile, was again disguising herself, this time in a more accustomed role as a woman. Prior to the Battle of Seven Pines, which began on May 31, 1862, (s)he morphed into a female Irish pie salesman named Bridget, with a brogue good enough that the Confederate Irish considered her one of the "rale ould stock of bog-trotters," and began collecting intelligence.

Two days later, McClellan addressed a wildly cheering army of men, explaining that, based on their successful body of work, they were finally about to march on Richmond. Two months later the army moved, but not in the direction the men had hoped. Edmonds noted that "the ominous fact that we turned our backs toward Richmond was very suggestive of a retreat." Soldiers reacted in one of two ways. "The men were deeply moved; some wept like children, others swore like demons, and all partook in the general dissatisfaction of the movement." Their unannounced destination was Newport News, seventy miles back in the direction they had come. "It was well for us that we did not know it then, or there probably would have been more swearing and less weeping among the soldiers."

Despite his accomplishments through several major campaigns as a spy and nurse, Frank Thompson didn't finish out the war. And he would have been shot had he tried. Edmonds and her male persona silently left the ranks after contracting malaria, choosing to be treated at a private hospital where matters of gender would not raise as many eyebrows as they would in an army hospital. In better health, she started to return to her regiment, but thought better of it when she noticed posters seeking information about the whereabouts of one Frank Thompson, deserter. She finished out the war playing the role of herself, ministering to the sick and wounded in a Washington hospital. She married after the war and had three children. Ultimately, her service was acknowledged and she received an honorable discharge and a military pension for her role in a small but passionate sorority.

Somewhere in the rolling hills outside of Sharpsburg, Maryland, was, or perhaps is to this day, an unmarked grave containing the bones of a soldier who wanted to remain anonymous. Edmonds understood; in fact, she dug the grave herself after administering to the soldier, who had suffered a mortal neck wound at Antietam. Something about the youngster caught Edmonds's attention and something about Edmonds gave the dying boy confidence. "I can trust you," the soldier said. "And I can tell you a secret. I am not what I seem, but a female. I enlisted from the purest motives, and have remained undiscovered and unsuspected. I have neither father, mother nor sister. My only brother was killed today. I closed his eyes about an hour before I was wounded; I will soon be with him."

Her last wish was to be buried off by herself, her secret kept for eternity. It would take a special person to be able to fill that request, and the chances of discovering such a person at that particular point in time might have been only a few out of a couple of hundred thousand. And yet, according to Edmonds's account, it happened. In a sea of men, on a field of honor, sister had found sister.

CHAPTER 5

The North Finds Its Hero, Briefly

In retrospect, not everyone in the North saw the First Battle of Bull Run as a disaster. "On the 21st July, 1861, the North lost the battle of Bull Run," wrote John Watts De Peyster, years after the fact. "But the rebels did not win anything but the possession of the field, for the gain was altogether with the North."

This would have come as news to residents in and around Washington, D.C., who had packed picnic hampers full of wine, cheese, and other goodies into their carriages and trundled down to the crossroads of Manassas to "tailgate" before the battle, much as they do today with their beloved Washington Redskins.

By day's end, of course, both spectators and the blue-clad main attraction alike were sprinting as one back to safe ground, soldiers chucking their weapons as they ran and carriages jammed together in accordioned waves of horse-drawn panic. In the first major land battle of the war, the novices of the South proved to be better than the novices of the North, and an initially tough contest turned into a rout.

But De Peyster's angle (and he was, and is, not alone in his thinking) was this: Bull Run was a cold slap to the psyche of the North, which up to that point had viewed the rebellion as more of an impending nuisance than an impending catastrophe. Bull Run, he said, ". . . cemented the free states; it awakened the people to the necessity of organizing a proper army; it taught the government that (it) could no longer trifle with events."

Watching from the sidelines at the time, a one-armed, aristocratic soldier of fortune named Philip Kearny wasn't so sure. One more defeat like Bull Run, he warned, the Union's flabby goose of a military might just be cooked.

Kearny was the wealthy son of a New York tycoon who had helped found the New York Stock Exchange. The elder Kearny had groomed his boy to be a force on Wall Street, a life the young man didn't want. The younger Kearny's call was to be a force on the field of battle, and despite a law degree and an inheritance of better than $1 million, he joined the U.S. Army and made himself into easily the best military man not to be on the field when the Civil War broke out.

Sporting an elegant van dyke matted to a hawklike face was Kearny in the saddle, holding his reins in his teeth and waving pistol and/or saber, the sight of which inspired poetry, even among the most well-intentioned writers. De Peyster wrote, but probably shouldn't have, in part because he was a cousin of Kearny:

No one who has ever studied the lineaments and expression of Philip Kearny, his carriage, his bearing on foot or

seat in the saddle, but must . . . acknowledge in their hearts
that his soldierly face and knightly person would look more
appropriate under the morion and the mail of Fra Moreale,
of Do Guesclin, or of Batard, or in the plumed hat lined
with steel, and polished breastplate of a Rupert, a Mon-
trose, or a Dundee; nor deem him in the saddle unworthy of
Sir Richard Vernon's glowing description of that "Imp of
Fame," who, on the field of Agincourt, so glorious to his
manhood, declared . . .

We get the idea. What's harder to understand is why the
North, so desperately in need of leadership, ignored such a talent.
The North had anticipated that it would crush the South like a
bug and get on with business as usual, and with capable leadership this dream might have been achieved. Instead, the North was
led by a virtual Who's Not Who of fighting men, for whom the
word "competent" was much yearned for but seldom achieved.
The North understood it had lost its best general when, after
much tormented soul-searching, Robert E. Lee threw his lot in
with his native Virginia. But as fortune would have it, the second-
best, third-best, and on down the line had also defected—or so it
seemed, as Lincoln discarded general after general, looking for a
hand that was at least bluff-worthy in the face of Southern talent.

Irvin McDowell had just blown an early advantage at the
First Battle of Bull Run and almost lost Washington in the
process. John Pope would muck up Bull Run redux. Joe Hooker's name would be remembered not for military skill, but for
the ladies of ill repute that lazed around his camp. Ambrose
Burnside was praised by contemporary soldier and later historian Ezra Carman as having "a fine row of teeth." Burnside
at least knew his limitations, and repeatedly tried to duck

Lincoln's attempted promotions. Out of options and excuses, Burnside rose to the top and commenced to lead his poor men into one slaughter after another. Wrote Carman, "It is not going too far to say that the Union cause would have received no hurt and (saved) much blood had Burnside's own estimate of his ability been accepted by the administration."

Benjamin Franklin Butler's occupation of New Orleans was so mean and corrupt that residents of the city had the general's bald and jowly countenance painted on the bottoms of their chamber pots. George McClellan was a supreme organizer, be it of military ranks or the never-ending oyster and Champagne parties he hosted on the Potomac, an activity he seemed to far prefer to any actual fighting.

Southern generals had such nicknames as "Stonewall" (Thomas Jackson) and "The Gray Ghost" (John Mosby). Northern generals had names like "Old Fuss and Feathers," (Winfield Scott) "Baldy" (William Smith), and (read into this nickname what you will) "Old Brains" (Henry Halleck). Nathaniel Banks lost so many battles and supply trains to Stonewall Jackson in the Shenandoah Valley that the Rebels took to calling him "Commissary Banks." Even the North's most bellicose nickname, "Fighting Joe" Hooker, was the product of a typo. The dispatch was meant to read: "Fighting—Joe Hooker attacks Rebels." Hooker in fact was a decent enough commander, who imprudently suggested that the nation needed a dictator, and the sooner the better. Lincoln got wind of the comment and told Hooker that he'd accept a victory and chance the dictatorship.

Yet the Union ranks were not without talent, and gradually that talent began to rise, even if it seemed at times that the North's best men were battling against the South and their own commanders at the same time.

In a war filled with ten million what-ifs, it's probably best not to dwell too heavily on Kearny's potential. Study of his career can arouse irrational exuberance in Northern partisans; it is all too easy to get caught up in the excitement and assume, probably wrongly, that with the stroke of a pen placing the army in Kearny's hands, the war would have been over in the late summer of 1862.

We see this now. No one saw it back when it mattered.

Though chivalrous and high-minded, Kearny was not a perfect man. His behavior was manic, his temper was legendary, his wit was acerbic, and his soul was tormented. He could drive most anyone, male or female, to tears with his chronic complaining. Impatient for the birth of his first child, he blew

One-armed Philip Kearny was known for holding the reins in his teeth and leading his men into battle—in the middle of a raging storm, often as not. (Courtesy Library of Congress) *Note: Kearny's name is misspelled in the print*

up at the calendar for not allowing the days to pass quickly enough. His psyche skipped from thunderstorm to thunderstorm, with rays of the warmest sunshine and icy currents of depression carving canyons in between the tumult.

But Kearny was the perfect soldier. Prior to the Civil War, Kearny studied tactics overseas at the famed cavalry school at Saumur, France; he rode gallantly in battle with the *Chasseurs d'Afrique*, where he earned the name Kearny le Magnifique; he drove Indians out of Oregon settlements; in the Mexican War he became known as the Hero of Churubusco, for a daring cavalry charge that cost him his left arm; and he returned to France and fought the Austrians, helping the French Imperial Guard capture a key spot on the battlefield at Solferino, toward the end of the second War of Italian Independence.

Kearny had followed and learned from the best commanding officers in the world. He was intensely patriotic to the Union cause and renowned for being able to organize rabble into fine fighting forces. His military genius and his bravery were unquestioned. Kearny had been pinned with the *Legion d'honneur* twice, once by the duc d'Orleans, and once by the Emperor Louis Napoleon himself.

With this on his resume, Kearny sailed home from Paris in 1861 and presented himself to the Union for service—and was turned down.

For all his success on actual battlefields, Kearny's political pedigree was not in order, and he had a reputation for selling out any commander or politician whom he deemed inadequate—which was just about all of them. Aside from the aging Gen. Winfield Scott, Kearny had few friends in high places. And while the South was basing its military leadership— Lee, Jackson, Stewart, Longstreet, Hill, Early—on merit, the

North was basing its military leadership on political party allegiance, congressional friendship, and West Point cliques. It is no overstatement to say that in Kearny's place among the North's generals were men whose chief military attribute was that of being, for example, a pro-Union Democrat.

It wasn't the first frustration Kearny had felt in the army, his primary quarrel with the institution being that there wasn't enough quarreling. In peacetime, he had spent dreary months under Scott doing little more than entertaining high-profile dignitaries, there being no hostilities at the time.

"Am I to spend my military career," he moaned, "as a highly placed flunky looking to floral decorations in banquet rooms, escorting visiting bores and dancing with the ugly wives and the clumsy daughters of foreign diplomats?" For the sake of Kearny and clumsy daughters everywhere, the Mexican War was about to commence.

This theater was vintage Kearny, as he led a daring, marginally irresponsible dragoon charge up to the gates of Mexico City. It was a fine sight. He'd raised the force of men himself and paid for their elegant attire and weaponry out of his own deep pockets. With the help of a Midwestern attorney he had outfitted them with one hundred twenty matching gray horses. As the charge played out, the commanding officer eventually called Kearny and his men back with a bugle—a serenade apparently heard by most all the horsemen but Kearny. (Kearny did admit later that he heard the bugle call, but frankly, waving his pistol and swinging his sword in a sea of enemy infantry was just too much fun.) Without his mates, of course, the action went against him, and as he was riding away, a cannon shot tore off his arm. Semiconscious, Kearny, asked which arm was gone. Informed that it was his left, Kearny nodded and said, "I envisioned this."

But despite this heroism, Kearny couldn't even get a gig with an outfit from his home state of New York a dozen years later. If the military establishment couldn't see Kearny's worth (in one instance he was told he could not be the leader of young men because he was divorced), the leading newspapers and citizens of the state could. "The lives of our fine young men are of less importance than the wishes of ward heelers and political leaders whose protégés have to be given consideration," said one frustrated New Yorker.

If Kearny was hated by the politicians, he hated them right back, loudly and publicly—which was part of the problem, truth be told. He raged at the "nincompoops and incompetents" who were chosen as officers, and he bellowed even more loudly at the men who were doing the choosing. Finally, a frustrated and disillusioned Kearny retired to his New Jersey mansion. "I have been traduced by intriguers," he said glumly. "What am I to do?"

If Kearny was disillusioned, so was anyone who had ever tried to lead the drunken, ragtag band of hoodlums and slackers that were collectively known as the First New Jersey, a military brigade in name only. Kearny's friends made a case to the governor that the one-armed solder might be the one person who could out-ornery the First New Jersey, but a number of political favorites were already in line.

Fortunately, for Kearny at least, the governor's decision was influenced and expedited by the Bull Run debacle. Suddenly the great soldier's marital status was irrelevant; Kearny was nominated to the command of the First New Jersey, but he needed the affirmation of the president. As it turned out this was not an issue, since the Midwestern attorney who had worked with Kearny to round up one hundred twenty gray horses many years before was a man by the name of Lincoln.

As brigadier general of the First New Jersey, Kearny took a gang of drunks and turned them into a ferocious fighting machine. Now they just needed someone to fight, which, given the paralysis of McClellan, was not a sure thing. Kearny spent the fall of 1861 drilling his New Jersey volunteers into one of the army's finest brigades, and wondering why no one else—notably McClellan—seemed to understand that there was a war going on. Where Kearny loved to brainstorm with his colleagues about great European battles and tactics, it seemed, as one officer wrote, that McClellan "acts as if he had taken the oath to some hidden and veiled deity . . . not to ascertain any thing about the condition of the enemy."

Kearny, by contrast, drew up multiple plans of battle that concentrated on booting the Confederates from the steps of the Northern capitol and pushing on to Richmond.

But, writes De Peyster, "Kearny's soldiership was always too prompt and energetic, not only for McClellan, but for those immediately over him in command. Had Kearny's advice been followed, Kearny's 'practical strategy' would have maneuvered the Rebels out of their insulting positions in front of Washington . . ." and pressed the battle southward.

Kearny relished warfare, which he viewed as a divine form of high culture. He was hard on his men, but he made sure they got the best food and equipment. He himself traveled in a carpeted wagon stocked with fine French wines and his own personal French chef. All was in ready for a glorious campaign.

Kearny waited. And stewed. His own personal water kettle of a temper was always on simmer, and it took little flame to boost it to a rolling boil. When he caught some of his men stealing chickens, an awestruck private observed that "the general cussed us out for ten minutes, maybe longer—and he never repeated himself once." Kearney stalked back to his headquarters grumbling that the one sure way to whip the South was to strategically place Richmond between his men and a henhouse.

To his credit, McClellan had taken the scared rats of Bull Run and turned them into a well-organized and well-drilled army "whose equal has never been seen in the Western world," said the general himself. Kearny wondered how he could know that this was true without seeing it under fire. If McClellan had a plan, he wasn't letting anyone in on it. Secrecy, Kearny noted dryly, was an asset in men of genius, but in McClellan it was "most unfortunate . . . Talent he has; genius he has not."

McClellan, stationed in Northern Virginia, was convinced the Rebel army just to the south was superior in numbers and artillery strength; rows of big guns poked out from fortifications near Centerville. Kearny received a directive to protect a railroad crew but not to approach Southern lines. He circumvented this restriction by leading his brigade toward enemy lines, only on the grounds that it was a necessary part of protecting the railroad crew. Amazingly enough, Kearny received information from an escaped slave that the Rebels were planning to evacuate their position. Kearny spread his brigade to make the Confederates think the army as a whole was approaching, and the South's orderly withdrawal developed an atmosphere of panic. Kearny's brigade captured rich caches of Confederate gear, which had been left behind as the South beat a more hasty retreat than it had originally planned. As Kearny's men sorted through the loot, it was the left-behind artillery that captured the volatile general's attention. They were nothing but logs painted black, known in the parlance of the day as "Quaker guns."

Kearny understood the truth; McClellan had been duped into thinking the South was dealing from a position of strength, when in fact, divisive action might have resulted in a swift Union victory. Short of that, Kearny believed that it was not too late for the North to catch up with the retreating Confederates and beat them all the way back to Richmond, using Virginia's wide, easterly flowing rivers to supply the army along the way. This was the point, in March of 1862, when a bold move (before Robert E. Lee had been elevated to lead the Southern army) might have had interesting consequences. But it was not to be. Wrote Kearny:

> *Instead of letting me and others push on after the panic-stricken foe and forcing him to fight a big battle and probably ending the war . . . McClellan has brought us all back. The result will be that the Rebels, thinking us afraid of a real, stand-up fight . . . will take daring action against us, while we strike timidly at them.*

McClellan, of course, didn't see it this way. His plan was for a tortured aquatic troop movement in the spring of 1862 ("conceived in weakness and crippled at birth," Kearny believed) to a finger of Virginia land flanked to the north by the York River and to the south by the James. The army was to eventually work its way up this peninsula to Richmond, but even getting troops to the drop-off point at Fort Monroe on the Chesapeake Bay proved to be a long, logistical nightmare. The inaction had Kearny toggling between deep bouts of depression (exacerbated by the death of his two-year-old boy back home) and volcanic disgorgements of hatred, generally directed at McClellan, although whoever was close by would serve. He had been promised that his brigade would lead the charge off the boat to capture Yorktown. Instead, Kearny disembarked to find a lot of men milling around and a lot of equipment hung up in the mud; McClellan, fearful of being outnumbered, had called off the frontal attack.

This was bad enough in Kearny's view, but worse was the revelation that once again the South had only a small defending garrison that, on the approach of the North, slipped away, no damage done. McClellan called this a "shattering victory," and doubtless there was more shattering going on at Kearny headquarters, where he had now been promoted to division commander but again found nothing to lead a command against. Kearny would not have been surprised to learn that Confederate commander Joseph Johnston had clucked to Lee that "only McClellan" would have failed to attack.

THE GUNBOAT CANDIDATE
AT THE BATTLE OF MALVERN HILL.

A cartoon lampoons McClellan as viewing the Peninsula campaign through a telescope from his safe perch. He calls to the troops, "Fight on my brave Soldiers and push the enemy to the wall, from this spanker boom your beloved General looks down upon you." (Courtesy Library of Congress)

Kearny finally got his chance in a pouring rain at Williamsburg, when his division was called up to assist Joe Hooker, who had made a good stand but was now feeling the pressure. Kearny arrived on the battlefield in timely fashion, only after he threatened to burn Union supply wagons if they didn't move out of his way. He found Union troops dazed and confused in the rain, smoke, and mist. He spotted a brigade standing around under some trees and incredulously asked why they were not engaged.

Because they did not know where the enemy was, they said. Here's how you find out, Kearny shouted, as he spurred his horse and rode a hundred yards across an open field and back. White puffs of smoke from rifles tucked in the opposite woods followed his course but only served to give away the Confederate position. Hooker's beleaguered men witnessed this crazy one-armed man risking it all and they knew the score. A cheer rang across the field, "Car-knee! Car-knee!" Kearny's presence was an inspiration unlike any other, wrote Kearny biographer Irving Werstein:

That day every soldier in the division saw Phil at least once, dashing across the battle line, standing in his stirrups, kepi on his sword tip, reins in his teeth—his staff officers close behind him. Somehow the knowledge that his general was running the same risks made a green private feel better.

His fellow officers, not so much. "Doesn't Kearny realize he's a general," his corps commander exploded. "A *general*, not a reckless shavetail to lead a bayonet charge." In part due to his bravado, Kearny's men would "walk through the gates of hell" for him, but events would demonstrate that the corps commander was not wrong.

The legend of Kearny grew. Confederate prisoners all wanted to know who the one-armed general was. In the heat of battle, a joyful Kearny would laugh with ease and instruct his men to "go in (to the fray) gaily." At Seven Pines, in a desperate situation and hemmed in against the Chickahominy River, a colonel asked where his men could do the most good. "Go in anywhere, colonel, go in anywhere," Kearny blithely retorted. "You'll find lovely fighting all up and down the line."

After capturing a Rebel headquarters, legend has it that a group of Union officers' action stalled as they contemplated a full bottle of whiskey, speculating as to whether or not it had been poisoned. An impatient Kearny blew into the room, grabbed the bottle, and chugged a few gulps before handing it back and saying that if he was not dead in fifteen minutes they should feel free to pass around the liquor, but in the meantime they better get to work.

McClellan continued to inch up the peninsula toward Richmond—the "Virginia Creeper," Kearny called him—until, potentially on the verge of a tremendous victory, he ordered a full retreat. Although this did not fall entirely on McClellan. Pinkerton agents had convinced him the enemy was 200,000 strong, a horrendous overestimate. Even so, McClellan does not get a complete pass; soldiers such as Kearny and Hooker guessed the truth and champed at the bit to advance. But with the Union— and maybe more importantly to him, his reputation and potential presidential run—hanging in the balance, McClellan did not feel as if he had the luxury of losing.

So with the spires of Richmond within sight, and the church bells within earshot, McClellan backed down the peninsula. The South, with Lee now having replaced a wounded Gen. Joe Johnston, pushed the attack and, even if it lost the battle, kept gaining ground. Disgusted and discouraged Northern soldiers called it "the great skedaddle." After a clear victory at Malvern Hill, McClellan ordered another retreat, leaving stunned men standing in a downpour, words having deserted them. Words did not desert Kearny. They never did. In perhaps his most famous harangue he threw his hat into the mud and pronounced:

> *I, Philip Kearny, an old soldier, protest this order for retreat. We ought instead of retreating to follow up the enemy and take Richmond. And in full view of all the responsibility of such a declaration, I say to you all, such an order can only be prompted by cowardice or treason.*

But Kearny, along with the others, obeyed the orders and slumped back toward the bay. Two months later, at Chantilly, a Confederate bullet put Kearny out of his misery. He was serving under Pope at the time, whose leadership was even more contemptible than McClellan's. "Are there only imbeciles to lead us?" he stormed, before galloping out in the dark to scout an enemy position. As usual, he was warned of the risk. As usual, he didn't listen.

Down in the mud, a few yards away, a slave girl trying to cross into Federal territory under the cover of dark heard the shots and watched the gallant general fall from his saddle. Except this wasn't a slave at all, but the Union's mistress of disguise Sarah Edmonds. "When I learned who was their victim, I regretted that it had been me instead of him whom they had discovered and shot," she wrote. "I would willingly have died to save such a great general. . . but he was taken while I, a poor insignificant creature was left."

The Southern shooters whooped and hollered and then fell silent. When he saw the officer fall, Confederate Gen. A. P. Hill scrambled to the site and held up a lantern. There was no joy in his voice as he said, "You've killed Phil Kearny; he deserved a better fate than to die in the mud."

Exactly how close he was to that better fate will never be fully known. Werstein wrote, "Almost at the moment when Kearny pitched to the ground, Secretary of War Stanton was signing papers promoting him to the rank of major general. In Washington a rumor was being started that Kearny was to replace McClellan as the Commanding General of the Army of the Potomac."

Thanks to Kearny's own impudence, he was finally gaining the respect he deserved, although he would never get the chance to employ it for the benefit of the Union.

CHAPTER 6

Paying For it All

E veryone has a pet "turning point" in the Civil War, the time
when the South's momentum flagged in the face of the North's
unrelenting industrial machine. For many, it's Gettysburg, when
Maj. Gen. George Pickett's infantry was blown to bits during an
unshielded attack on the Federal's center. For others, it's the death
of Stonewall Jackson, or a set of misplaced orders that gave away
the Confederate's battle plan prior to Antietam.

But for *The Ascent of Money* author Niall Ferguson, the true
and little-celebrated turning point occurred relatively early on,
in the spring of 1862, when Union Flag Officer David Farragut's
gunboats blasted their way past two Confederate forts at the
mouth of the Mississippi River, then sailed into New Orleans
unopposed. From that point, the South's finances, and the
South itself, were doomed.

Of all the celebrated causes of the Civil War, cotton might
be the most overlooked. The labor-intensive crop necessitated

great numbers of slaves; its hunger for nutrients necessitated great amounts of land. Cotton was a political as well as an agricultural phenomenon. It was an economic powerhouse that fed the mills (and the hardscrabble laborers) of the industrial North and of Europe; three-fourths of France and Britain's cotton came from the South, and the textile industry supported as much as a quarter of Britain's population. Some assumed cotton made the South bulletproof. "You dare not make war on cotton," James Henry Hammond, a senator from South Carolina famously snapped at New York's William Seward. "No power on earth dares make war upon it. Cotton is king."

Provided it could get to market, of course.

As a champion of decentralization, the South had no unified taxing authority, so it needed to seek out creative financing alternatives. Its own people somewhat voluntarily paid for the early part of the war by purchasing $115 million worth of bonds, but Southern liquidity was rather quickly tapped out. Southern financiers waved war bonds under the noses of European investors as well, with little result until, Ferguson writes, the South came up with an "ingenious trick:" It would back up its bonds with its most valuable possession—a fluffy, white form of collateral.

The bearer of the "cotton bond" might have his doubts about the validity of the Confederate States of America, but this was immaterial if he could redeem the paper for cotton at a low prewar price.

Of course the South needed land not just for cotton, but to grow food for hungry soldiers, so planters were encouraged to cut back on cotton in the name of grain production. This was not necessarily a detriment to the cotton-financed war, because the less cotton that was produced, the more it (and its bonds) was worth. Supply and demand never fit a cause so neatly. Indeed, the South, hoping to pressure Europe into the war, moved to restrict cotton exports altogether, an act that prompted mill closures and food riots in Britain.

Had all gone according to plan, Britain might have capitulated and thrown its power behind the South, and foreign investors might have jumped into the market for cotton bonds with both feet. The South, Ferguson observed, was one cotton harvest away from glory.

But at the critical point in time when the South needed to restock European ports with fiber, ships found themselves blocked at New Orleans. For Confederates, it was a financial disaster. British mills began to find other cotton sources to the east and recalled hungry workers to their looms.

In turn, investors became skeptical of the South's ability to deliver the goods as promised by its bonds. "The Confederacy had overplayed its hand," Ferguson contends. "They had turned off the cotton tap, then lost the ability to turn it back on." The South's chief financial instruments were tagged with that dreaded term "speculative." The South needed the support of Britain and France—but more desperately needed the support of Britain and France's bond houses, and that didn't happen.

Still, money had to be raised somehow. Aside from lives lost, the financial costs of the Civil War were astounding. By 1863, the U.S. government estimated it was costing $2.5 million a day. It did not escape notice in Washington that for the money spent on the war, it might be cheaper for the government to buy up and free all the slaves in the border states. All told, the South's costs would top $2 billion, the North's more than twice that (pensions paid to soldiers eventually totaled more than the war itself).

The South printed its own money, of course, with ultimately poor results. When Southern armies were attempting to win the hearts and minds of Marylanders in 1862, they graciously offered to pay farmers in "graybacks" for the crops and livestock they consumed. The parsimonious people squinted at the strange looking Confederate bills, wrinkled their noses, and indicated, thanks anyway, but they would be happier to be paid in gold. It was sound judgment. While inflation affected the North to a degree, in the South hyperinflation whittled the value of a Confederate dollar to a few pennies or less. The North was more than happy to help in this inflationary spiral (estimated at 4,000 percent) by printing up counterfeit greybacks and dumping them in the South. By the time of the Battle of Gettysburg, the Maryland farmers' suspicions had been realized. A Pennsylvania shopkeeper complained mildly that raiding Rebels had paid him for his wares, but "it was in Confederate scrip, which now has a value chiefly for purposes of curiosity."

From a sketch by a Union prisoner of war, southerners auction off a scarce $25 gold piece, a response to hyper-inflation and metal shortages in the Confederacy. (Courtesy Library of Congress)

The war affected currency, and currency affected the war in other, more curious ways as well. With all metals going into the war effort (or being hoarded by citizens and speculators) there was a serious shortage of coin. So pressed were New York City grocers to make change that they began substituting two-penny ferry tickets for legal tender. In response, government and private enterprise alike printed the equivalent of paper coins known as "shinplasters," so named on the grounds that the script was so cheap it was more productive to add a fillip of starch and water to the paper and stuff the biomass into one's socks to warm the ankles. One irate reader of the *New York Times* smelled a rat. He saw a time when millions of dollars worth of shinplasters would be printed, but not redeemed by dishonest establishments. "And who will be the losers of these millions? Who but the innocent?" he stormed. Indeed—some manufacturers liked the idea of printing their own money so much that—until labor and government got involved—they began printing up payroll. The North and South might have differed on slavery, the territories, and state rights, but on the matter of shinplasters they spoke with one voice. The Richmond Whig railed against the "uncouth and ridiculous looking" notes from Southern banks, necessitated by the hoarding of actual silver, nickel, and copper change. Papers in both the North and South offered the same advice: Refuse to accept the shinplaster.

By 1864, nerves were understandably frayed from the hostilities, and money played a central part in the tensions. With elections at hand in the North and the Lincoln administration's discomfort with a growing stalemate, the Federals became more malicious in the Shenandoah Valley of Virginia. Soldiers were given permission, if not encouraged, to burn and pillage private homes, which enraged, among others, Confederate Gen. Jubal Early. The Virginia farmers, Early decided, were in need of financial compensation, and Early was happy to take his traveling marauding show on the road. He began to turn to Northern towns in search of either cash or fiery acts of retribution. He didn't particularly prefer one over the other.

Confederate Gen. Jubal Early engaged in epic missions of revenge for damage to civilian property in the Shenandoah Valley perpetrated by northern commanders Phil Sheridan and George Custer. After the war he packed up and went to live in Canada. (Courtesy Library of Congress)

In Hagerstown, Maryland, the rumors got there long before the Confederates did. Said the *Hagerstown Torch and Light*:

"Rumor succeeded rumor, and the last was always more
alarming than its predecessor, and no two of them were exactly
the alike, but the fact that the Rebels were on their way to pay
us a huge visit was sufficient in itself to cause alarm."

Everything that was valuable and portable was shipped out
of town. By newspaper accounts, the waiting seemed to cause
more angst than the actual Confederate occupation. When
Early's surrogate, Gen. John McCausland, and his troops finally arrived on July 6, "The council was politely told by this
polished representative of our 'Southern brethren' that if the
demand was not was complied with, within a limited time, the
town would be laid in ashes."

Southern soldiers set up shop in front of the court house
and demanded clothes and $20,000 in cash. Townsfolk im-
mediately complied with the clothing part, and if the Confederates ever got around to wearing the wardrobe in total
it must have been quite a show based on the multiplicity of
styles and patterns and colors that were forthcoming. As it
was, something of an orgy of haberdashery broke out, with
grinning Rebels trying on elegant hats and flannel shirts and
rather disappointing Hagerstown civilians who, frankly, had
been expecting more élan. "There was none of that 'modest
dignity' in the man of which we have heard so much—none of
that polish and Southern refinement so peculiar to the man of
the South," sniffed a disappointed *Torch and Light*.

Still, there was the matter of the cash and on this point
Southern honor ruled the day. The Hagerstown Council,
while certainly aggrieved and all, seemed a bit curious about
the $20,000, which the papers said was "a feather" compared

to the mischief that could have been done. Indeed, this was less than $300,000 in today's dollars, barely what it might cost the parks department to install some new tennis courts. It was later determined that Hagerstown was the beneficiary of a typo and that Early's agents were supposed to demand $200,000. Any potentially delicious private conversations afterward in the Southern camp ("You asked them for *how* much?") have of course been lost, but to a good Southerner word was bond and Early would not be so dishonorable as to break an agreement by demanding another $180,000.

After leaving Hagerstown, Early's men plundered Boonsboro and Middletown before they pressed up against the outskirts of Frederick, Maryland, and menacingly delivered a grocery list to the town fathers, who offered up supplies of bacon, flour, salt, and coffee. Not only did the Confederates uncharacteristically fail to pay for the goods, Early followed up with a ransom note demanding—having learned from past mistakes—$200,000, which the town bankers willingly delivered in baskets to a waiting Southern wagon. Meticulous to a fault, the Confederates gave the bankers a receipt. (The city repaid this sum to the banks in 1951 and has been trying unsuccessfully to get reimbursed by the federal government ever since.)

After briefly threatening Washington, Early next sent a raiding party north to Chambersburg, a small Pennsylvania city a few miles across the Maryland border, with the orders that its residents should pony up $100,000 in gold or $500,000 in currency as payment for Union damage in the Shenandoah Valley. If Chambersburg didn't pay, it was to be burned.

The raid was led by McCausland, who brushed aside light Union resistance and entered Chambersburg's square on the morning of July 30. He took breakfast at a local hotel and ordered his men to fetch the town leaders, including a prominent attorney named J. W. Douglas, who read over Early's orders and commenced to deliver the news to the townsfolk—many of whom laughed at him for his trouble. "When I spoke earnestly about the terrible alternative they said [the Confederates] were trying to scare us and went into their houses," Douglas later recalled. He tried another street, with the same result. The Pennsylvanians by this time were used to, if not entirely comfortable with, Southerner encroachment. Several other forays, including the march to Gettysburg, had not left Chambersburg particularly the worse for wear. In 1863, one woman—getting her first glimpse of Robert E. Lee in person—asked the great general for his autograph. "You want the autograph of a Rebel?" a perplexed Lee replied. Confederate boys were likewise puzzled to see young men their own age in Pennsylvania who were not in uniform. They chatted with their counterparts, telling them that back home, anyone who could serve did.

This time, the atmosphere was not as casual. Most of the town's cash and wares had already been shipped out, in consideration of Chambersburg's proximity to the Mason Dixon line. The town elders said that not only did they not have the requested funds, it was rather ridiculous to ask for such an amount. The response was swift. Southern soldiers barged into private homes, piled up the furniture, and applied the torch. "The burning was executed in a most ruthless and unrelenting manner," wrote eyewitness Benjamin Shroder Schneck. Every building in the downtown went up in smoke, save for the local Masonic lodge, which survived out of the professional courtesy of Southern Masons. For the North, this was an act of terrorism, plain and simple, never mind that it had been provoked. Vivid accounts of screaming men, women, and children, along with photos of the smoldering city, made the rounds in Northern newspapers. Elderly and infirm residents had to be dragged to the safety of nearby fields. Soldiers swilled all available liquor and robbed individual citizens. When McCausland died more than sixty years later, Northern newspapers still referred to him as "the Hun of Chambersburg."

Early, for his part, had no regrets when he recalled the raid in 1887. "The act was done in retaliation for outrages committed by Gen. David Hunter in the Valley of Virginia . . . This was in strict accordance with the laws of war and was a just retaliation."

But these raids were not the most bizarre of the Southern money grabs. That honor goes, oddly enough, to Confederate attacks on one town in eastern Maine, and on another in northwest Vermont, so far from Southern territory that there are only about four frost-free months in the year.

Canada was in the awkward position of being a refuge for runaway slaves and slaveholders alike. It wasn't uncommon for escaped Confederate prisoners in the North to make a run for Ontario, where, in theory, they might freely walk the streets with the same men they had owned prior to the war. Canada was also home to Confederate spies and desperadoes with little to do but draw up crackpot schemes against the Union. At this point, Sherman was thundering toward the sea, a muddy-trousered Grant was en route to Richmond, the Confederacy was broke, and the Southern cause was desperate, if not hopeless. The time for first downs had passed; the situation called for a Hail Mary, one last dramatic game-changer. If peaceful, sleepy towns more than five hundred miles north of the Mason-

Dixon line could be sacked, it might cause a nationwide panic, it might force the North to relocate its troops, it might . . . well, it was worth a shot.

On a late-July morning in 1864, a tall, rough-looking character named William Collins stuffed a Confederate flag into his pants, the idea being to fly it over Calais, Maine, once the far-afield Yankee outpost had been captured. Whether or not there would be a town left to fly the flag over was a bit up in the air, since his gang planned to burn it to the ground, but that detail could be worked out later. Collins and two accomplices began the raid by hitting the Calais National Bank, with the expectation that as many as fifty comrades would arrive shortly thereafter by sea. If this band of brothers existed at all, they never showed. Worse for the bank robbers, the secret of the attack had been poorly kept, and Calais had armed men waiting on every street corner. When Collins made a move for his pistol, the teller sounded an alarm, and state guardsmen rushed to the rescue.

Another one of these Southern soldiers active in the North was a fresh-faced young man named Bennett Young, who didn't turn twenty until a couple of years into the war. After escaping from an Ohio Federal prison camp and scampering to Canada, Young hatched a plan to attack the unsuspecting town of St. Albans, Vermont, on the northern shores of Lake Champlain. Young's force of twenty fellow Kentuckians burst into the town on October 19, much to the initial amusement of townsfolk who had trouble believing their eyes. Rebel gunfire convinced them of the seriousness of the matter, and the town mounted a counterattack that chased the bandits out of town, but not before they had killed a local citizen and heisted $200,000 from St. Albans's banks. Writing for *America's Civil War* magazine, Ron Soodalter said the Confederates brought with them bottles of an incendiary fluid known as Greek fire that was peddled as the napalm of its day. Lobbed against wooden buildings, it was supposed to set the city afire and provide cover for Young's company as they retreated back to Canada. It did neither. Nor was the Canadian border any meaningful deterrent to the visibly agitated residents of St. Albans, who spurred their horses right through this international stop sign and apprehended Young at a Canadian farmhouse. Young protested to the mob that it was in violation of British neutrality law, a theory the angry men saw as interesting but not of any particular relevance to the matter at hand. Young was beaten and tossed in a wagon for transport back to Vermont, saved only by a passing Canadian officer who convinced the mob to follow traditional channels. At the end of the day, most of the Confederates and about half of the cash were recovered— although not before Canada's policy of protecting Rebels nearly touched off an international incident.

Banks, or course, were not the sole purveyors of cash— Union soldiers could often be counted on to have a couple of bucks; Confederates capturing a Union soldier might not ask questions about the enemy's position, but would instead query as to whether the soldier had recently been paid. On the same day that Young had attacked St. Albans, a Yankee soldier by the name of Thomas Douglas had been shot in the face and thigh at Cedar Creek in Virginia. As he lay immobilized on the battlefield, men under the command of the aforementioned Jubal Early approached and, Douglas later wrote to Early in appreciation, "asked how long since I had been paid off." Finding no currency on him, they stole his canteen just as Early himself approached the group. "I looked earnestly at you and said to you, 'Do you allow a man to rob another of the last drop of water he possesses?' Straightaway you rode up to [the thief], made him give up my canteen, and filled it yourself with water for me. 'Now,' said you, 'Get away to your command.'" At least one of the Huns of Chambersburg could be a teddy bear.

CHAPTER 7

The North's Shadow Cabinet Member

For the anti-slavery North, the dawn of 1862 did not represent morning in America. Abolitionists had been hanged, the government had been booted from its own property at gunpoint, its armies had been routed, and its generals seemed incapable of organizing a two-horse parade.

Even some early, trifling victories in 1861 in what would become the state of West Virginia served to do little but elevate the career of Gen. George B. McClellan, the commander who was to come to set the gold standard for treading water.

Perhaps the most meaningful event the North had managed by early 1862 was a naval victory at Cape Hatteras that served to reinforce its Atlantic blockade of Southern ports. Otherwise there was little to cheer, and those who predicted that it would get worse before it got better would prove to be correct.

Winds of confusion buffeted all levels of government, civilian and military; the Southern child that the North believed was in need of a good, quick spanking had itself unexpectedly risen up and wrested the rod from the parent. For days after the First Battle of Bull Run, Federal soldiers had straggled back into Washington, D.C., where the country's leaders watched them stretch out in front of the White House and commence to get drunk—an appropriate if temporary response to events. No one seemed to have any good answers or operative plans.

Out of this mess rose an individual with a keen legal and tactical mind, a clear vision of what the Union represented, and, as Mark Twain would have characterized it, "a pen warmed up in hell." A former slaveholder, this patriot helped beat back the secessionist movement in Maryland and wrote opinions that legitimized President Lincoln's handling of the national emergency before venturing out West and hatching a military scheme that gave the Union its first meaningful land victories and ultimately turned the tide of the war.

The timing was fortuitous, even critical. Bumbling Federal forces were giving Europe no good reason to stay neutral and refrain from throwing its lot in with the South, which its mills depended upon for the South's prodigious cotton crops. A desperate Congress—not sold on Lincoln's martial leadership—created a Committee on the Conduct of the War and named a firebrand senator from Ohio, Ben Wade, as its chairman. Wade was an indelicate specimen and a fierce abolitionist who believed that Lincoln's tepid views on freeing the slaves exposed the president's "white trash" (his words) roots. Possessor of a sharp scowl and sharper tongue, he was not shy in his criticism of the Union's military leadership, which in 1861 was ineptly clawing at air like a cat being held by the scruff of the neck. Wade's committee impatiently reviewed plan after plan as proposed by the military, none of which had any prayer of providing the required immediate battlefield gratification.

"Just at that time," Wade later wrote, "Colonel (Thomas) Scott informed me that there was a plan which, if executed with secrecy . . . would save the national cause."

Wade burst into Lincoln's office and demanded to know if such a plan did indeed exist. Well, yes, Lincoln said, but it wasn't a military plan; it had in fact been sketched out by a civilian. Wade was about to shear a pin. If it was a good plan, he wanted to hear it, forthwith. But there was a bigger stumbling block, Lincoln said, for "it is not only the work of a civilian, it is the work of a woman."

This juicy vignette plays out in a 1952 biography by Sydney and Marjorie Greenbie titled *Anna Ella Carroll and Abraham Lincoln*. Could it possibly be accurate? Could the great War Between the States really have been won by a girl? There is certainly a good case to be made, whether or not it's in the hands of a decidedly pro-Carroll biography as the Greenbies' work must be categorized.

Getting to the bottom of the mystery that is Anna Ella "Anne" Carroll is no easy chore. Her critics, assuming they bother giving her the time of day at all, discount her contributions and suggest that her talents largely began and ended with a flair for self-promotion. Even in this century, historians have wrinkled their noses at her perpetual harping for pay and for being "shrilly and tiresomely" (the words of historian E. B. Long in 1975) championed by suffragettes and even by relatively modern-day feminists. But if Carroll had not stood up for herself, it's fairly certain that no nineteenth-century

male historians would either. Today, it is difficult not to conclude that she was a remarkable woman by historical standards, not just the standards of her day. Scholar, schemer, law
student, diplomat, writer, tactician—Anne Carroll is something of a Hillary Clinton in a hoopskirt. Carroll's acknowledged accomplishments should by all rights put her at least at
the level of a Mary Chesnut or a Clara Barton, war-era women
of great merit who were polite enough to confine their activi-
ties to the male-approved-worlds of writing and nursing. In
a time when women were denied the vote, Carroll's modern sympathizers suggest that men were fully capable of wiping her record from historical records, helped out by, as the
Greenbies put it, "wicked and malicious historians" who—it
gets dicey here—have failed to question documentation that
doesn't exist.

Carroll's detractors suggest that no record of her more con-
troversial (alleged) accomplishments can be found. Carroll's
supporters say that this proves their point; we know enough of
Carroll to know that she should show up (in letters and docu-
ments) where she doesn't, which is evidence of a conspiracy.

But what we do know is intriguing enough. Carroll was
born in 1815 and grew up the daughter of a planter on Maryland's Eastern Shore. The family owned slaves, but the operation was more of a commune than a business; profits suffered
because the family could not bear to sell any of the expanding
slave family to the infamously cruel Southern cotton fields.
Her father, Thomas Carroll, served as governor in 1830–31,
and as a child she soaked up law, politics, and current events
at her daddy's knee. "As soon as she really knew her letters
he turned her loose in Coke and Blackstone," the Greenbies
wrote. "She learned to assist him by taking down the big law

books and finding the passages he wished to use in one of those interminable arguments about the law and the Constitution which were meat and drink to Southern legislators."

By the time she was ten years old in 1825, Anne was acting as her father's secretary, sorting his mail and scanning newspapers for articles that demanded his attention. Visitors with business before her dad would chortle merrily as she spouted some passage from a law book, much as they might be amused with a dog balancing a biscuit on its nose. But the laughter began to fade as they learned she could be trusted to recount an important issue to her father if he was away when they came calling.

Carroll's spare time was spent not so much with needle and thread, but in poring over maps, learning the rivers of the region, and waiting on the wharf for news of foreign military adventures. To grow up in a border state was to grow up in a field of gray—there were no clear answers about slavery or federalism as there were farther to the north or south. Therefore it's understandable that Carroll's views did not evolve along predictable lines. Tyranny was to be fought, but loyalty demanded faith in the Union. Slavery was wrong, but so was freeing slaves into a world in which they were ill-prepared to cope (it was illegal to simply free slaves in Maryland prior to the war, so Carroll went into personal debt so that she could buy freedom for her own slaves).

While antebellum society blocked a career as a lawyer, Carroll discovered that a woman could still be an advocate before the bar of public opinion, and she became a pamphleteer and publicist for causes that ranged from political careers to the plight of downtrodden sailors. Her books included anti-Catholic screeds, for which the Know Nothing party was famous, but also advocated scientific and industrial missions, including proposals for a railroad to the Pacific.

Anna Ella Carroll was, by necessity of the day, a player behind the scenes. But because she remained behind the scenes it is difficult to tell how much of her story is valid—or if there may be even more to her tale that can never be revealed. (Courtesy Maryland Women's Hall of Fame / Maryland Commission for Women and Women Legislators of Maryland)

Carroll gets credit for helping elect Thomas Hicks, a friend of her father's, governor of Maryland—an act that just might have been more important for the Union than anything she did or didn't do later on. Despite Southern sympathies, Hicks was solidly pro-Union and as we have seen, helped prevent Maryland from seceding, assisted by Carroll's pro-Union propaganda.

There is also no question about the collective pedigree of Carroll's friends and confidants, which included presidents Pierce, Tyler, Fillmore, and Buchanan, as well as Henry Clay, Salmon Chase, Stephen Douglas, Edwin Stanton, Jefferson Davis, Winfield Scott, and a host of others. So Carroll was either a political mover and shaker, or one of the nation's more impressive gadflies.

But for all this, it was the events of 1861 that stirred the pot.

Carroll informed Thomas Scott, by then assistant secretary of war, that she was bound for St. Louis to visit relatives and research a paper on presidential war powers. Scott, she wrote, "urged me to go" and survey events in the war's Western Theater. Like everything else for the North at this point in time, events were not positive. Military leaders, according to the Greenbies, were involved in little more action than aimless shoulder-shrugging as they tried to cook up a plan that would split the Confederacy in two. Conventional wisdom held that this was best accomplished by control of the Mississippi River, but there were clear problems. As Carroll sat in a St. Louis library doing her research, Southern sympathizers—unaware of her employer, it seems—bragged about Southern defenses along the river in detail specific enough to convince Carroll that a Northern assault would be suicide. She also winced when she saw the North assembling a flotilla of low-slung gunboats that, if disabled, as they almost assuredly would be, would float helplessly on the Mississippi's powerful current straight downstream into the Confederate's hands. Carroll needed a river that flowed north. She began to ask around. And the sources she sought out were the same sources that taught her about river navigation many years before in Maryland: steamship pilots.

Relying on her life long fascination with geography, watercourses and railroads, Carroll began to cobble together a plan. The Tennessee River did indeed flow "up," and the Tennessee/Cumberland River watersheds were lightly defended. Even better, a pilot named Charles Scott—who confirmed Carroll's fears about the Mississippi—said gunboats would be able to navigate the Tennessee River all the way to Muscle Shoals in Alabama. From there, it would be a relative hop to the Alabama and Tombigbee rivers that flowed south to the sea. Such an offensive, Carroll wrote in a detailed report to Scott, would also cut the legs out from under Southern defenses on the Mississippi, threaten Memphis and Nashville and disable the key railroads running west that supplied Confederate armies with food.

Those who saw the plan, Lincoln included, were said to be ecstatic, and with good reason: Forts Henry and Donelson on the Tennessee and Cumberland rivers were indeed captured by a relatively uncelebrated officer whose demand of total capitulation earned him the nickname "Unconditional Surrender" (U.S.) Grant. The successful implementation of Carroll's plan, or whoever's plan, was reason enough to set church bells to ringing throughout the North. In the West, the Yankee nose was under the tent. Kentucky was saved for the Union, Tennessee was opened to attack and Southern supply lines suffered a crippling blow.

The only matters of this success to be settled were ones of payment and credit.

Long contended that the Tennessee Plan was "patently obvious," and that it did not need the likes of Carroll to point it out, seeing as how plenty of other people had the same thought. And Carroll, who faced financial troubles for much of her life, subtracted from her legacy, or at least gave ammunition to her detractors, by repeatedly badgering Congress for compensation. In 1881 Congress considered a bill to grant recognition and a military pension to Carroll, but, according to the Maryland State Archives, the bill "mysteriously disappeared" following the assassination of President Garfield. She did eventually win a small military pension, but her cause was taken up by suffragettes who equated a lack of female recognition with a lack of female voting rights. Carroll's legacy has smoldered ever since. Francis B. Carpenter in 1864 painted Lincoln, surrounded by cabinet members, reading the Emancipation Proclamation. But there's one empty chair, and propped up against it are maps of the South. To some, this is the smoking paintbrush, the clandestine acknowledgment of Lincoln's secret cabinet member who drew up the blueprints for the North's first significant land victories. To others, sometimes an empty chair is just an empty chair. "[I]t can be said with surety," Long wrote, "That Anna Ella Carroll was not a 'hidden' figure of history, maliciously hidden, that is, by chauvinist historians. She was and will remain a minor figure . . . with slim importance."

But in 1874, in a letter to Carroll, Senator Wade's view was somewhat different:

"If ever there was a righteous claim on earth, you have one. I have often been sorry that, knowing all this, as I did then, I had not publicly declared you as the author. But we were fully alive to the importance of absolute secrecy . . . As the expedition advanced Mr. Lincoln, Mr. Stanton, and myself frequently alluded to your extraordinary sagacity and unselfish patriotism, but all agreed that you should be recognized for your most noble services, and properly rewarded for the same."

CHAPTER 8

Racing Locomotives

As maligned as armies of the North were in the first year of the war, it's worth noting that Union troops were capturing towns in the Deep South a year after Fort Sumter. Huntsville, Alabama—which supplied eight generals to the fray, four of whom fought for the North—was captured on April 11, 1862.

Union Maj. Gen. Ormsby "Old Stars" Mitchel was, befitting the nickname, an astronomer at the Dudley Observatory in Albany, New York, when the war broke out. He'd been a classmate of Robert E. Lee at West Point, and published the nation's first monthly magazine on astronomy. Owing to his work in his chosen profession, a crater and a mountain range are today named after him on the planet Mars.

But in the spring of 1862, his division was advancing, more or less, to a Confederate concentration at Corinth in northeastern Mississippi. His primary orders were to protect Nashville, but he had the authority to make trouble wherever trouble in the region might be made. After capturing Huntsville, Mitchel eyed eastern Tennessee, which was rich in resources and people who remained loyal to the Union. Time would tell that Mitchel had a propensity for jumping the gun; he was unable to hold Huntsville, and he had inadequate support to make inroads into eastern Tennessee. But his dreams did not go unshared.

Ormsby "Old Stars" Mitchel authorized events that led to the Great Locomotive Chase. He briefly quit his day job as an astronomer to fight the Rebels. (Courtesy Library of Congress)

James Andrews was a Midwestern house painter and singing coach turned Union spy. He fixated on trains early on, figuring that if he could steal one he could go on a mad tear, cutting telegraph wires, burning bridges, pulling up rails, and in general disabling Southern communications and transport. Mitchel liked the idea. He would attack Chattanooga after James had stolen a train in Georgia and obliterated Confederate lines of support that could be called to the defense of the city.

James and twenty-four men in civilian dress wandered, a few at a time, off into the countryside, the cover story being that they were headed to sign up for service on the Confederate army. It was, the Rev. William Pittenger, then of the 2nd Ohio, later wrote, "a romantic and adventurous plan." And not without pitfalls. A couple of the men were approached by southern locals and dutifully spelled out their cover story—at which point they were dutifully marched to the closest recruiting station and pressed into service.

Rain poured down as the rest of the men made their final plans, and with the mud that reliably led to delays came the news (erroneous as it would turn out) that Mitchel's troops would be stalled an additional day. So the expedition was bumped back from Friday, April 11, to Saturday, April 12. No one at the time could know the cataclysmic difference this small change in plans would make.

Having arrived in Georgia, each man was given one last chance to back out. None did, even though they found themselves on a wet, rainy morning surrounded by Southern soldiers at every turn. At Kenesaw Mountain they collectively gulped at the sight of a vast Confederate encampment, which provided "a painfully thrilling moment." At the Kenesaw Station, the train stopped and the crew and many passengers got off to eat breakfast at the cafe. Andrews's men got to work. They uncoupled the passenger cars as the undercover engineers and firemen darted into the locomotive and the balance of the men tumbled into a boxcar behind the tender. An armed Confederate guard stood a few feet from the train, but his eyes simply couldn't make his brain adjust to the unfolding events in any way that made sense to him, and by the time he had pulled himself together enough to act, it was too late. Andrews's engineer threw open the valve, and the *General* (pre-Civil War locomotives were given names rather than numbers) bolted ahead in front of a stunned audience that had no idea what was happening. What was about to happen were seven hours and eighty-seven of the wildest miles in United States history.

Andrews had carefully studied the road's timetable, and knew he would meet two southbound freight trains. But they would be expecting the northbound *General* as well, and so long as everyone kept to schedule and availed themselves of the proper sidings there should be no problem. Once the second freight had passed, it was full steam ahead to the key bridges leading into Tennessee. They were to be burned, at which point—any possible pursuit being cut off—Andrews anticipated a leisurely chug to Chattanooga. Everything was falling perfectly into place.

The rogue band of rail men was in good spirits and good order as they began their mission. They cut telegraph wires and took on some cross ties to be used as kindling for future bridge fires. Cool as cucumbers, they filled up with wood and water at Southern stations, calmly stating that they were on a special mission carrying powder for General Beauregard.

But the raiders didn't bargain on the outrage and determination felt by two men back at the Kenesaw Station named

William Fuller and Anthony Murphy, who were members of the legitimate crew of the *General* and very much wanted their train back. They had taken off after the vanishing train on foot and then on a co-opted handcar, which proceeded slowly but surely until it spilled gracelessly into a ditch thanks to a rail that had been dislodged by the departing thieves.

Meanwhile, this job of rail springing took longer than it should because the raisers did not have the proper tools. But the suspense "possessed just enough of the spice of danger in this part of the run to render it thoroughly enjoyable," Pittenger recalled. As they chugged into Etowah Station, they noticed an old beater of an engine on a siding, the *Yonah*, which was serving out its golden years in the employ of an iron mine. The *Yonah*'s steam was up, but the threat seemed minor, and disabling it would have attracted too much unwanted attention. Had this been Friday instead of Saturday, the logic would have been sound.

The crew waited out the second southbound freight, but as it came into sight the men were dismayed to see that it was displaying a red flag, which indicated another train still to come. And *that* train had a red flag of its own, which would lead to more downtime that the men of the *General* couldn't afford. Andrews stepped in and asked station masters the reason for all these freights running south. After all, Beauregard was an impatient man and needed his powder. The answer, Pittenger noted, "was interesting, but not reassuring."

Word had spread that Mitchel's army was (as originally scheduled) approaching Chattanooga, and the Confederates were evacuating as many supplies from the town as possible prior to the attack. The wait continued. They didn't know who might be after them by now. They didn't know who in the gathering crowd of their enemies knew what. The men in the boxcar, who had no clue what the problem was, grew anxious. Andrews had only been able to give them a brief word: Be ready to fight. "So intolerable was our suspense that the order for a deadly conflict would have been felt as a relief," wrote Pittenger. At last, the final freight pulled in, and with unspeakable relief the crew of the *General* was off again, leaving the increasingly inquisitive and suspicious crowd behind.

Back at Etowah Station, two excited and exhausted men ran panting up to the platform, with a wild story to tell and some sharp shouted orders. The *Yonah*, whose career as an industrial workhorse was winding to a well-earned retirement, was about to become a pursuit vehicle for a band of Confederate commandos.

At a less intense pace now, the *General* was stopped on the road north as the men set about cutting telegraph wires and pulling up rails. Again, it was a time-consuming process performed as it was, without proper tools. At this crucial juncture, the men were startled by the scream of a locomotive whistle to the south, where no train should have been. This increased the amount of interest the crew had in popping the rail, and with one superhuman effort it was dislodged, the equal and opposite reaction sending the men tumbling down a bank.

The pair of intrepid men who were the rightful bearers of the *General* slammed on the brakes of the *Yonah* in time to avoid disaster, but there was no time to try to patch up the Yankee's vandalism. They abandoned their locomotive and once again set off at a sprint, leaving their team of commandeered soldiers behind. Even at the trot, they would soon be making better time than the *General*, which became snarled in southbound traffic, her crew peppered with questions that were getting harder and harder to answer with any degree of believability. Finally the traffic cleared. The next station was nine miles distant, but an express was due from that direction at any time. Word was that it was running a bit late. It was a gamble Andrews had to take.

The *General* gave it everything she had. Engines in those days had to sweat to break twenty mph, but Pittenger believed they covered the nine miles in nine minutes, arriving just as the conductor of the express was pulling out. Hearing the shriek of the whistle, the conductor of the express stopped and backed up on the siding far enough for the Federals to get mostly, but not entirely, past. Enough strange things were happening that Saturday morning that Southern antennae were up and functioning with full force. It took Andrews's best performance to date. *General Beauregard* needed his *powder*, dammit! The express allowed them to pass.

Fuller and Murphy had not counted on the Yankees' ability to slip past the express. Instead, the *General* had gotten away, with nothing but open road between it and the safety of Mitchel's troops. One more stop was needed—to burn the Oostanaula Bridge—and the rest of the journey, Pittenger reckoned, would be "simple manual labor, with the enemy absolutely powerless."

That harmonious dream was again shattered by a screaming whistle and a train bearing down on them "at frightening speed." Backward. What the . . . ?

Fuller and Murphy had had their own problems with congestion, until they grabbed a southbound locomotive named the *Texas* and ran her to the north as fast as she would go. Sure enough, the *General* was stopped ahead, and just coming into rifle range. Two more minutes were all the Yankees needed to spring the rail. They didn't have it. All piled back into the train and the race was on. Andrews still hoped to stop and burn a bridge, and to buy the time he uncoupled a car from the *General* to block the way—and watched incredulously as his pursuers barely slowed but slammed into the car and pushed it back the way it had come.

The Confederates couldn't pass, but they could press the *General* until it ran out of fuel and water. Or so they thought. But Andrews still had some tricks up his sleeve. Every so often he'd toss some cross ties onto the tracks, compelling Fuller and Murphy to stop and clear the rails. These measures delayed Fuller and Murphy enough that the crew of the *General* was able to twice take on wood and water and cut the wires after passing each station. The two most effective measures would have been to pop a rail or burn a bridge, but there wasn't time for the former, and the day was too wet for the latter. Pittenger recalled:

> *Thus we sped on, mile after mile, in this fearful chase, around curves and past stations in seemingly endless perspective. Whenever we lost sight of the enemy beyond a curve we hoped that some of our obstructions had been effective in throwing him from the track and that we would see him no more; but at each long reach backward the smoke was again seen, and the shrill whistle was like the scream of a bird of prey.*

Trains of that day were not intended for such breakneck speeds, especially if there might be something in the way. On a particularly sharp curve, Andrews's men threw down a tie, knowing that there was no way for their pursuers to see it and stop in time. Sure enough, they hit it square. Sometime after the fact, Fuller admitted that it caused quite a jolt, and swore that the train popped up in the air and settled, roughly, back on the rails. At this point, several of the Confederate soldiers who were along for the ride said they believed they would like to stop and get off, but "their wishes were not gratified."

In the end, the raiders were doomed for want of the railroad equivalent of a simple claw hammer, which would have allowed them to quickly and easily pull up spikes and sabotage the road. In one last, desperate effort, the men tore up half of the last wooden boxcar and threw it in the tender for fuel, setting the rest on fire and releasing it from the train under a covered, wooden bridge. They rooted hard as they could for the bridge to catch before their pursuers caught up, but it didn't happen. The *Texas* pushed the flaming car out of the bridge and onto the next siding. Without time to stop for wood and water, the *General*'s miles were numbered. The raiders milked nearly all the steam they could out of the *General* before throwing her in reverse toward the oncoming pursuit and scrambling from the scene. In one last fillip of bad luck for Andrews, there wasn't enough energy left in the *General*'s boiler to crash the *Texas*.

The manhunt for the raiders was, Pittenger said, "prompt, energetic and successful." All were captured and tried as spies. Andrews and seven others were hanged, while the rest were exchanged or escaped. Many were among the first recipients of the newly created Medal of Honor.

The Great Locomotive Chase has twice been retold in film, as a silent-film comedy in 1926 called *The General*, and thirty years later in a Disney movie starring Fess Parker. The silent film was a Buster Keaton production that was a box office disaster roundly panned by the critics. That was then. Today, like the Great Locomotive Chase itself, *The General* is considered to be a classic.

CHAPTER 9
Civil War Ammunition—A Blast from the Past

Every fight gained a reputation for something or other, and the September 17 Battle of Antietam was specifically known as an "artillery hell." In an infantry fight, men die one bullet at a time. In an artillery fight, men die in bulk. A Maryland newspaper reporter, who liked to keep track of who killed whom, finally gave up. Watching an advancing line of men, he would see a segment of it simply disappear like a missing tooth in a grisly grin. But there were so many batteries on so many hillocks firing so many rounds that it became impossible to figure out which company should get credit for the successful shot.[1]

---

[1] Soldiers liked to keep track of, and brag about, their successes. After Shiloh, an officer dryly noted that he had been "searching diligently for the past five days for the man who *didn't* kill General Johnston."

People believed the terrible losses at Shiloh that past April were as bad as it could get. Antietam counted the same number of casualties, 23,000, as Shiloh, but it took place in one day instead of two. It was a record that would not be topped.

Artillery was the one of the reasons; the rolling hills bristled with five-hundred big guns. But the technology of guns, large and small, was fast outstripping commanders' ability to keep their ranks safe from wholesale slaughter.

Major League catcher and wit Bob Uecker once remarked that the best way to catch a knuckleball was to "wait until it stopped rolling, and then walk over and pick it up." A well-thrown knuckleball does not spin as do more traditional pitches, making its course impossible to predict for pitcher and batter alike. Such was the case with most pre–Civil War weapons, which had smooth barrels that spat out round balls to be buffeted unpredictably on the air currents.

The old flintlock muskets that were prevalent in the South at the outbreak of the war were colorful relics. Their erratic behavior is best illustrated by the prodigious amount of slang spawned by the weapon: Go off half-cocked; shoot your wad; flash in the pan; lock, stock, and barrel. The Union had some bad guns of their own; one Pennsylvania regiment reported getting some cases of Belgian rifles packed in grease that could only be shot once before requiring "repairs to one or the other, the gun or the man."

Rifling—filing long, spiral grooves into gun barrels to spin the bullet—was a technology had been around for centuries, but rifles had not proved to be terribly effective in the field of battle. To work, the muzzle-loaded bullet had to snugly contact the grooves, and consequently it took some time and effort to ram the bullet down the barrel into place. Such a project might be suitable for snipers or for shooting squirrels, but on the field of battle, time was more than money—it was the difference between life and death.

Still, smoothbores had an accuracy of only about fifty yards, whereas rifles could be depended upon at five times that distance, and some even had a puncher's chance at a halfmile. This is theoretical; under the pressure of battle, there was seldom time to compose an artful, accurate shot at great distances. The great cry of officers to their men was "Aim low!" an antidote against the odd propensity in battle to point the weapon at a forty-five-degree upward angle.

Barely a dozen years before the outbreak of the Civil War, a French army captain, Claude Minie, had hollowed the bottom out of a regular bullet, and a new standard for ammunition had been set. When the gunpowder detonated, the sides of the bullet flared outward like a hoopskirt in an updraft. It was easy to load, but the expansion of the lead solved the problem of contact with the barrel. In the 1850s, the U.S. War Department in general, and specifically Lt. J. G. Benton, an ordnance expert at the Harpers Ferry arsenal, was experimenting with these new projectiles.

In a controlled test, the future of the round ball was sealed: "At four-hundred yards, the flight of the round ball was so wild that all further practice was suspended," a War Department report stated.

That same report experimented with all manner of bullets and barrels, technologies that would be in place for the start of the war—for the North at least; the South was still mainly armed with antiques, but captured both Federal guns and gun-manufacturing equipment in quantities that compromised the Union's advantage.

This technology had a profound effect on strategy and tactics, and, it might be argued, helps in part explain why—

even though the North developed the gun technology and had it in greater amounts—the South was the prime beneficiary.

The Minie ball was a tremendous advantage for the defense. Previously, when an attack was initiated from a half mile away, there wasn't a whole lot for the defending infantry (stationed, perhaps, behind a stone wall or in a sunken road) to do but watch and wait until the attackers got to within a couple hundred feet of the defensive works. A charge across a vast, open field was not suicide then. Aggression typically paid off. But with highly accurate rifles, such a charge might be under constant infantry fire from the first step.

The South had its aggressive actions to be sure, but in sum it was fighting a defensive war against Northern invaders. These new long-range weapons fit them perfectly. During the signature action at Fredericksburg, Virginia, in late 1862, the South settled in behind a stone wall and picked off Federal soldiers like tin cans as they clamored up from the river. So horrific were the odds for the North that the Southern boys wondered if they were fighting a war or committing mass murder.

By contrast, some of the South's most notorious defeats, at Gettysburg and Franklin to name two, could be blamed on over-aggression.

Long-range weapons favored cautious, defense-oriented generals such as Gen. James Longstreet, considered by some to be the finest corps commander for either side. On the Peninsula campaign, as McClellan threatened the outskirts of Richmond, the notoriously polioesque commander kept playing defense and winning—at which point he would retreat, play more defense, and win again. It's a bit of a stretch, but not much, to say that McClellan succeeded often enough that soon he was right back in Northern Virginia, where he had started out from in the first

place. During Gen. Ulysses Grant's Virginia campaign, Lee repeated McClellan's win-and-retreat pattern of two years earlier.
Grant (who did have the advantage of attrition on his side as
well) lost his way to the steps of the Confederate capital.

By then, it was dawning on commanders that strong defensive earthworks were the key to if not victory, then at least to
not losing. When Grant settled in outside Petersburg, the two
armies settled into nine months of what one general described
as "a mutual siege." Lee's army had to be starved out of position. But this stalemate was an ominous precursor to the trench

By the end of the war, both sides were digging in and lobbing cannon
and mortar shells at each other. The stalemate at Petersburg was a harbinger of the trench warfare of World War I. (Courtesy National Archives)

warfare of World War I, where armies battled back and forth for years over possession of a few extra feet.

Another peek into the future was provided by the Spencer Repeating Rifle, which was almost too advanced for its own good. It could fire six or seven shots in about the time than it took to load and fire the standard rifle of the day. The Battle of Hoover's Gap in central Tennessee in the summer of 1863 was and is overshadowed by the somewhat simultaneous action at Gettysburg and Vicksburg, and perhaps that's why its significance was lost. In order to prevent Confederate reinforcements from being sent to Vicksburg, U.S. Col. John Wilder's "Lightning Brigade" blew through the gap with a blaze of firepower that seemed all out of proportion to the men behind the guns. Southern officers looked searchingly at each other: What could the Federals have? With no clue about the repeater, the Confederates finally assumed they had been overwhelmed not by a brigade, but by the entire army of the Cumberland, and proceeded to hightail it fifteen miles to the rear to Tullahoma.

"I think the Johnny's are getting rattled," wrote a Union soldier to the folks back home. "They are afraid of our repeating rifles. They say we are not fair and that we have guns that we load up on Sunday and shoot all the rest of the week." One group of Southern boys surrendered to a Michigan cavalry unit just so they could see the repeater up close—or so the story went.

The soldiers were convinced, but not the U.S. War Department, which was concerned that such a fast rate of fire might tempt soldiers to, well, fire fast. This might contribute to a waste of ammunition and to a man's failure to put enough care and consideration into his shot. This "they can shoot it fast, or they can shoot it right" nonsense sent the frustrated inventor, Christopher Spencer to seek an audience with President Lincoln. Lincoln, as he so often had to do, overrode the hang-ups of his underlings. But it could have happened much earlier. Failure to adopt the Spencer sooner was, wrote historian Bell Irvin Wiley, "one of the major tragedies on the Union side."

Big-gun technology was not advancing as rapidly, but the weapons were still impressive. Today we oft look at the scattered sampling of cannon that is standard fare of battlefield parks everywhere, and see a militaristic version of *Antiques Roadshow*. This wasn't the case in the war, of course. Each new Napoleon, Parrott, or Whitworth, its freshly painted wheels gleaming, its iron hardware or bronze barrel glinting in the sun, would have seemed every bit as modern and wondrous as an Abrams tank seems to us today. Each gun had its personality. A Whitworth could lob a shell a mile and a half with accuracy. Its loading mechanism was flawed, however, and it became one of those guns that would kill in front and cripple behind. The North generally couldn't be bothered with them; soldiers could tell when they were being used against them, however, because the shells produced a horrible shriek that could be heard above the general roar of war.

Good gunners, the expression had it, could—unless unnerved by the tension of war—knock the bottom out of a flour barrel from a mile away. And the setup was no less impressive.

A standard battery might be comprised of six guns that it took seventy to one-hundred men and nearly that many horses to operate. A two-wheeled cannon and its two-wheeled ammunition chest would be pulled by a team of six horses, and was not nearly as cumbersome as it sounds. The outfit was forty-three feet long and could turn in a forty-three-foot circle. The standard televised artillery reenactment—a big old draft horse deliberately lugging a cannon into place—is useful from a symbolic standpoint but bears little resemblance to reality. Instead, the piece would more likely be pulled by a team of fine athletic Morgans that could supply speed that draft animals could not. During battle, a battery would thunder into position, horses at a full gallop, cannon and caisson wheels bouncing high in the air and pinwheeling rooster tails of mud as high as a house. An experienced artillery team could set up and have the first shot off in a grand total of forty-five seconds.

Yet even the most advanced technology of the day could have its low-tech moments. For the Confederates especially, ammunition wasn't always plentiful. When cannonballs were short, it became necessary to chop up sections of a split rail fence and ram the wood into the barrel. At one point during the Battle of Antietam, Confederates resorted to firing sections of iron rail. This irregularly shaped projectile provided Union soldiers with some memorable moments, one for the uncharacteristic sound it made screeching through the sky. The second was that, unlike round projectiles, there was no predicting where these rails would bounce when they hit the ground. They would bound along helter-skelter and a soldier could never assume it wouldn't change course in a blink and come straight at him.

A full record of all the stuff ever jammed down the barrel of a cannon can never be constructed—most devastating at shorter ranges was the canister shot, which was basically a flimsy tin can jammed full of metal shards. When fired, the tin would disintegrate and a nest of deadly projectiles would fan out and rip large holes in enemy lines. Just about anything was fair game for canister grist. At Gettysburg, Winfield Hancock was struck by enemy fire. Painful as the wound was, he took great joy in noticing that his flesh had been pierced by a nail. The desperate Confederates, he believed, had run out of traditional ammunition. In fact, the shot had not hit him at all. It had hit his saddle and driven into his leg a nail that fastened the layers of leather together.

The weaponry technology advanced by the Southern side primarily came courtesy of two brothers who, if you were to ask a little boy, just might have had the two best jobs in Confederacy: One was in charge of gunpowder, the other in charge of bombs.

The Rains brothers, according to an extensive survey in the *Civil War Times*, did not seem to be close (they were separated by fourteen years and before and after the war lived across the nation from each other) and appear to have come by their incendiary careers independently. The younger brother George had perhaps the more conventional and more crucial job of the two and was responsible for producing the South's gunpowder. He scoured the confederacy in search of nitrates, taking them where he could find them, whether it was in limestone caves, company latrines, and residential outhouses. The residents were not universally enthusiastic about this particular aspect of the war effort, the connection between fertilizer and bombs not being as familiar as it is today. His state-of-the-art works in Augusta supplied the South with 3 million pounds of the finest gunpowder ever produced. Without George Rains's genius for powder, the South might have had to depend on imported gunpowder shipped in on blockade-runners, never an ideal form of supply. In a war in which everything else was in short supply, powder was the one commodity that was absolutely essential to have in quantity, and without Rains it is possible, if not probable, the South would have run disastrously short.

George's brother Gabriel began the war in the field as a brigadier general, a position in which he was not an overpowering success. He was quickly ushered by the Confederate hierarchy into a job where train wrecks were a good thing, not a bad thing—his assignment was to invent explosive devises to sabotage Union transport. Gabriel happily began to cook up an arsenal of what were then called torpedoes, but would be recognizable today as mines. He also concocted a Wile E. Coyote and Road Runner–like assembly of booby traps, most notably a bomb disguised as a chunk of coal that would explode when unwittingly shoveled into the boiler of a train or ship. Rains planted his mines in roads and in poorly defended Southern harbors. He would brag that, armed with his "torpedoes," a gang of workmen and couple of mules could stop an army.

His progress, however, was slowed in a couple of unforeseen ways. Along with all the other things it lacked, the South had no wire. The blasting cap or fuse (made famous by Ben Franklin a century prior) depended on wire to set off the primary charge that detonated the main charge. So Rains assembled a team of female thieves to cross enemy lines in search of wire; they hit the mother lode when they dredged a length of wire-rich cable in the Chesapeake Bay.

Worse, there was no small amount of discussion on both sides as to whether the mines were ethical. McClellan cried foul, and even the South's own Longstreet forbade their use in his command. The North threatened to march Southern prisoners in advance of their columns, and on at least one instance lashed a Confederate soldier to the bow of a ship until he disclosed the location of the mines. Finally, the South concluded the mines were okay for defense, but not simply as a way to inflict a few more random deaths on the enemy.

The mines did their best work in Southern harbors, sinking a dozen (and perhaps several dozen) Union ships. If nothing else, the psychological effect was significant, and sea captains became reluctant to go anywhere near Southern ports. The South discovered it

Gabriel Rains was a Southern master of explosives. Armed with gunpowder and a cunning mind, he developed coal-shaped bombs that would go off when shoveled into the boilers of enemy ships. (Courtesy Library of Congress)

could even dump empty barrels into the rivers with good effect on deterring skittish pilots. Not all Northern sailors were put off by the presence of the mines, most famously Union flag officer David Farragut who, in Mobile Bay, turned them into a historical and pop cultural icon when, warned of the mines, he snorted, "Damn the torpedoes, full speed ahead." Throwing caution to the wind, he sailed into the sea of bobbing bombs. It might seem funny to us now, but apparently his crew was not amused at the time, holding their breath and clenching all applicable muscle groups each time they heard the clap of a fuse being activated by the hull of their ship. Farragut was lucky; mines that had been floating in the salt water for any amount of time would corrode, one of their primary shortcomings in the days before stainless steel.

Another incendiary shortcoming was the occasional unreliability of the help. A flotilla of mines was prepared at one of Rains's factories to keep the Federals from steaming up the Mississippi River. A slave known as Old Pat was in charge of dispersing the floating bombs and sent along in a wagon full of weaponry. But either Old Pat was one of those people who does not have a mind for details, or his heart wasn't in "The Cause," because he neglected to anchor the mines to the river bottom and they all floated harmlessly out to sea.

In the 1932 obituary of another slave, Louis Carroll of Bamberg, South Carolina, an independent account of Confederate bomb-making came to light, this one an effort at designing a more conventional torpedo. Carroll, then a boy, would help his owner, Dr. Francis Carroll, affix a bomb to a hollowed-out six-foot oak log six inches in diameter. The explosive-packed log boat was propelled across the pond with a coiled spring, and apparently it was hell on stumps on the opposite shore. But in a demonstration before Charleston authorities it drew mixed reviews. The newspaper reported (with no apparent sense of irony): "The boat would correspond to the present-day submarine, except that it traveled on the surface, which was its apparent weak point."

Like many of the South's schemes as the war wound down, it was a plausible idea, but somewhat ahead of its time.

CHAPTER 10

A Foreigner Joins the Fight

The potato famine that extended into 1853 drove thousands of Irish out of agricultural turmoil there and into political turmoil here. By 1860, America's political parties were a mess, as they fragmented, coalesced into new parties such as the Americans and the Know Nothings, and then splintered all over again. By then, technology had helped kill off the Whigs; railroads and telegraph worked against that party's strategy of telling people in the South one thing, and people in the North another. Whigs were done in by communication much in the way that some politicians of today have been done in by Twitter.

American political parties had incentive to bring immigrants into the fold; men of power got two advantages in one, herding workers off to their factories and securing their votes in the process.

These men were technically free; in many ways their position was only marginally better off than captive labor in the South. Children had no protection from hard labor. Wages were so trifling that survival, one economist wrote, depended on "ruthless underconsumption." Living conditions were squalid and crowding in some parts of New York was said to rival Calcutta.

European immigrants were generally opposed to slavery, but at the same time a bit antsy about how the flood of additional labor—should the slaves be freed—would affect their economic situation. Still, patriotism to their new land eventually won out for many of them, and perhaps 140,000 men signed up for military service more or less straight off the boat. Most went with the Union, but certainly not all.

A young orphan named John Rowlands suffered a miserable upbringing in Wales, spending his formative years at an abusive workhouse before jumping a ship to New Orleans as a teenager. There, Rowlands caught the attention of a wealthy trader named Henry Hope Stanley who treated the boy as his own son. He groomed the young man in business and became the father Rowlands never had. In tribute, Rowlands took the name of Henry as well as the Stanley name.

The newly anointed Stanley wound up running a store in a rough-and-tumble county in Arkansas, where in 1860 talk of secession was all the rage. The immigrant viewed politics as "too dry," and only read the local papers for their shipping and commerce news. But increasingly, news of the secession and impending war could not be ignored. Without much luck, Stanley tried to get it through his head that the merchants and business associates in Cincinnati were now to be considered his "enemies."

Still, the entire county got war fever and it eventually swept up a reluctant Stanley—but only after he received a package from an unnamed girl that included a set of women's underwear. This was a tactic of Southern fire-eating women, designed to shame reluctant fellows into battle by raising questions about their gender. "[I]nflamed as the men and youths were," Stanley wrote, "the warlike fire that burned within their breasts was as nothing to the intense heat that glowed within the bosoms of the women. No suggestion of compromise was possible in their presence. If every man did not hasten to the battle, they vowed they would themselves rush out and meet the Yankee vandals. In a land where women are worshipped by the men, such language made them war-mad." He knew enough to enlist.

As a recent immigrant fighting for the South, Stanley was something of an oddity, but making matters worse was his complete disinterest in politics—he needed to learn Southern politics on the fly from his fellow soldiers as their feet blistered under the strain of their first lengthy march. War made for teachable moments, such as the instruction that it was OK to go out and steal food from Unionists. "Secretly, I was persuaded that it was as wrong to rob a poor Unionist as a Secessionist; but the word 'foraging,' which, by general consent, was bestowed on such deeds, mollified my scruples."

The men spent the winter of 1861- 1862 in winter quarters, fighting only bad weather, poor food, and flu. When Forts Henry and Donelson on the Cumberland and Tennessee rivers fell in February—the North's first significant land victories—the troops were hustled by foot and rail to a place that became known as Shiloh on the Tennessee River, with the idea of stopping the successful advance of an army under the command of Maj. Gen. Ulysses S. Grant.

Everything up until "Shiloh, Bloody Shiloh" had been child's play. Dangerous, to be sure—a fellow could get hurt—but nothing on the scale of Shiloh, where rows of men were dropped in their tracks, courtesy of two massive armies opposite each other standing, pointing, and shooting. After Shiloh, nothing would be a total shock. Before Shiloh, no one had a clue. Certainly not Stanley:

> *Day broke with every promise of a fine day. Next to me, on my right, was a boy of seventeen, Henry Parker. I remember it because, while we stood-at-ease, he drew my attention to some violets at his feet, and said, "It would be a good idea to put a few into my cap. Perhaps the Yanks won't shoot me if they see me wearing such flowers, for they are a sign of peace." "Capital," said I, "I will do the same." We plucked a bunch, and arranged the violets in our caps. The men in the ranks laughed at our proceedings, and had not the enemy been so near, their merry mood might have been communicated to the army.*

The troops stood in rank for half an hour prior to sunrise, as Southern commanders took care of last-minute details. Then forward, through field and wood the men marched, anxious and curious at once, for many had never experienced anything beyond a light skirmish. They didn't know what to expect. They didn't know how much farther they had to march before meeting the enemy. They didn't know—a roar of gunfire erupting from the left interrupted their daydreaming, and Stanley knew at least one regiment had found action. Within minutes it was his turn. "There was another explosive burst of musketry, the air was pierced by many missiles, which hummed and pinged sharply by our ears, pattered through the tree-tops, and brought twigs and leaves down on us. 'Those are bullets,' Henry whispered with awe." In an instant, the world as they knew it disintegrated around them, in a sheet of sound, flame, and smoke. As Stanley looked his comrades over, there was no sign of patriotism now, just survival. "[I]t was impossible for me to discover what they thought of it; but, by transmission of sympathy, I felt that they would gladly prefer to be elsewhere."

The miracle of Shiloh, in some regards, is that it wasn't worse. But storms of projectiles aren't conducive to concentration and a lot of men, hearts pounding, loaded and fired, aiming only in the general direction of the enemy. This was typical. In the chaos, soldiers were known to pack round after round into their weapons without tearing open the powder, dutifully ramming home bullets that would never fire. A horrible embarrassment it was to forget to remove the ramrod from the barrel before pulling the trigger, sending it flying across the battlefield.

Nor was it easy to see the target, for the thick smoke of spent gunpowder that hung over every battlefield. Stanley said he could not see the faces of his enemies, and was only aware of a haze of blue across the field as he and some members of his company took shelter behind a fallen log and poked their guns through a fifteen-inch gap between the timber and the ground. On one side of him, curiosity got the better of a soldier who popped his head over the log like a prairie dog and was immediately greeted with a bullet square in his forehead. Slowly, "he turned on his back and showed his ghastly white face to the sky." On the other side, a soldier stretched "as if to yawn" and turned toward Stanley, his face destroyed by a lucky shot that had traveled under the log and lengthwise through the man, the ball finally lodging in his chest.

> *But it was a terrible period! How the cannon bellowed, and their shells plunged and bounded, and flew with screeching hisses over us! Their sharp rending explosions and hurtling fragments made us shrink and cower, despite our utmost efforts to be cool and collected. I marvelled, as I heard the unintermitting patter, snip, thud, and hum of the bullets, how anyone could live under this raining death. I could hear the balls beating a merciless tattoo on the outer surface of the log, pinging vivaciously as they flew off at a tangent from it, and thudding into something or other, at the rate of a hundred a second.*

A shell mangled young Henry Parker's foot and left him wailing for his company to wait up. But, of course, waiting was not the plan. By single steps or full-out charges, the Confederates were pushing back the stubborn Federals and slowly but surely winning the field. In the middle of the advance, Stanley was knocked senseless by a bullet that hit him in the belt buckle. He would not regain his faculties until early in the afternoon, when he scrambled back to the ever-advancing front.

The Federals had been caught that morning sleepily boiling their coffee and leisurely pulling on their pants. That part of the Confederate plan at Shiloh had worked perfectly. As the Southern army advanced it overtook the Union tent cities frozen in the time in which their residents had been so rudely awakened. Clothes and blankets were strewn everywhere and Southern

DISCOVERY of the SAGE of CHAPPAQUA by H.M. STANLEY.

After the war, Horace Greeley ran for president against Ulysses Grant and lost. The great newspaper editor retreated to his weekend getaway, where he became known as the Sage of Chappaqua. John Rowlands, aka Henry Stanley, left the Civil War early and went on to become a journalist, among other adventures. In this cartoon from 1872, Stanley comes across the ever-more reclusive Greeley in a jungle. (Courtesy Library of Congress)

soldiers happily traded in their antiquated muskets for the latest U.S. Army–issue rifles that had been left behind. The Confederates called off the attack as darkness approached, and they dropped their exhausted selves beneath the Federal tents and dined on captured Federal rations of biscuits and molasses. Those who were still alive went to sleep believing they had won a great victory.

They had, but they hadn't. As disastrous as the day had been for them, the Yankees caught a couple of breaks.

Confederate Gen. Albert Sidney Johnston was killed early in the afternoon, leaving the South in the hands of Gen. P. G. T. Beauregard, who did not have a clear idea of Johnston's tactical plan. Second, by 9 AM, two Federal divisions occupied a forward field on a slightly sunken road and for seven hours absolutely refused to budge, no matter what the Rebels threw at them. The position wasn't strategically important, but Beauregard became obsessed with it and, rather than bypass what would become known as the Hornet's Nest, he charged it unsuccessfully as many as fourteen times. For the Federals, the Hornet's Nest had bought them enough time.

That night a merciless thunderstorm added to everyone's discomfort, and as Gen. William T. Sherman dragged himself back to headquarters he came across Grant sitting under a tree and contemplatively smoking a cigar, the pouring rain dripping off the brim of his soggy hat. "Grant, we've had the devil's own day," Sherman said. Grant solemnly agreed. Then he took a big long draw on his cigar and blew out a cloud of pungent smoke before adding, "Lick 'em tomorrow, though."

The Confederates awoke in the morning to a new, unwelcome deck of cards. The time bought by the Hornet's Nest and the desperate Union defense had allowed 15,000 reinforcements to move into place at Pittsburg Landing and now the North had a strength advantage approaching 2 to 1.

The soldiers in Stanley's regiment made a brief advance before a swell of advancing blue changed their minds. Unfortunately, no one told Stanley, who was leading the advance; he turned to discover Union troops where his comrades had been just a minute before. The young immigrant was now a prisoner of war.

Although, through his Southern indoctrination, he had considered himself to be among the best of the rabid fire-eaters, Stanley was open to compromise as circumstances made necessary.

> *On the way, my guards and I had a discussion about our respective causes, and, though I could not admit it, there was much reason in what they said, and I marvelled that they could put their case so well. For, until now, I was under the impression that they were robbers who only sought to desolate the South, and steal the slaves. But when the Southerners ... began to seize upon government property, forts, arsenals, and war-ships, and to set about establishing a separate system in the country, then the North resolved that this should not be, and that was the true reason of the war. The Northern people cared nothing for the 'niggers,' — the slavery question could have been settled in another and quieter way, — but they cared all their lives were worth for their country.*

Along with a number of other forlorn prisoners, Stanley was sent off to prison camp where, due to a multiplicity of miseries, "we were soon in a fair state of rotting, while yet alive . . . dead to everything but the flitting fancies of the hopeless."

There were no blacks in Wales, and Stanley for the life of him could not understand how a race of Africans could intercede between "white brothers." His allegiance remained primarily with the South on this matter, but after six weeks in the hellish conditions of Camp Douglas, he was not going to allow principle to stand in the way of his right "to die in the fresh air." He swore an oath to the Union and signed on to a Federal artillery squad, becoming one of a handful of men who fought on both sides. On reaching Harpers Ferry, (West) Virginia, however, the diseases Stanley had been exposed to at Camp Douglas caught up to him. He was discharged from service in June 1862, and, near death, struggled to make his way north to Hagerstown, Maryland. He was taken in and nursed back to health by a family three miles north of Sharpsburg whose house, unbeknownst to them, would in another ninety days be sitting smack on McClellan's right flank during the devastating Battle of Antietam.

Stanley went on in life to become a journalist; in his autobiography, he devotes only three chapters to the Civil War, a pity since he was such a marvelously descriptive writer. His writing career took him around the world, and in 1871 he found himself in the African bush surrounded by a friendly, he hoped, tribe of natives. Out of a grass hut stepped a weary-looking white man with a long gray beard and a blue cap.

Henry Stanley offered his hand and uttered four words that have echoed through history:

"Dr. Livingstone, I presume."

CHAPTER 11

Horses: Backbone of an Army

Fifteen years after the war, the shots may have ceased, but the North and South were still arguing over their horses. In an 1878 letter to *The Nation*, Confederate Gen. Richard Taylor chided Northern horsemen for wearing protective breastplates and strapping themselves to their horses to keep from falling off. In New England, he alleged, "horsemanship is an unknown art." This lit a fuse under Northern cavalryman J. A. Judson, who felt the need to drop this bomb:

> *People in the North certainly do not ride horseback as universally as they do South, and for the good reason that as we here are half a century in advance of most of that region in civilization, as a consequence among other things we have good carriage roads everywhere where we haven't steam transportation, so that horseback riding, save as a recreation, is unnecessary.*

Communication speed was not then what it is now, and Taylor was dead by the time Judson's letter in reply was published, so there was no need to separate the two as they threw gloves and paced off ground with their pistols.

The plight of the horse—his sheer numbers, his numerous duties, his nutritional demands, his struggles, and his impact—might be one of the more severely underreported parts of the war's history. The average horse in service of the Civil War lasted somewhere between four and eight months before dying from wounds, disease, or exhaustion. More horses died in the war (1 million) than men (618,000). After the Battle of Gettysburg, Lee's army of Northern Virginia included 6,000 sick or injured horses. "What made us heart-sick," a soldier wrote, "was to see a stray cavalry or artillery horse, galloping between the lines, snorting with terror, while his entrails, soiled with dust, trailed behind him."

But they were the backbone of the armies, and a quartermaster in charge of horses had to line up some serious product. It would not have been remarkable for the horses in one cavalry division alone to require ten tons of hay in a single day. One single cannon required a team of six horses to haul the gun and ammunition chest, while another team hauled more armaments and spare parts. The army diet for a working horse was fourteen pounds of hay and twelve pounds of oats a day. Pasture was not a substitute, because fresh grass didn't contain enough calories. Hay arrived by the freight car.

Though it took an average of five rifle shots to bring down a horse, it was a popular target during battle. Putting a team of horses out of commission effectively crippled a big gun. And being harnessed together, one thrashing horse could wreck a team and tear apart any member of the artillery team who happened to become tangled in the leather. Soldiers would have to pull their pistols and shoot the team in total before the dying horse kicked apart man and machine.

Horses were a tempting target, since they were the engine that ran the war machine. Here, Confederates assess the loss of a team and a caisson knocked out by a Federal artillery shell. (Courtesy National Archives)

Along with the mighty draft horses of the supply trains and the swift fighting horses of the cavalry, thousands of general utility horses were needed for officers and for pulling ambulances. Moving an army of men was bad; moving an army of horses was a nightmare. When Gen. Robert E. Lee invaded Maryland in 1862, a set of his secret orders fell into Union hands. Armed with this knowledge, swift action on the part of Gen. George McClellan might have quite literally divided and conquered the Rebels on a picturesque plane known as Pleasant Valley. But as the Union supply trains lurched west, they got hung up in hopeless animal gridlock at a crossroads in the small city of Frederick.[1]

A Southern officer once remarked that Confederate ground troops teamed with Union artillery could beat any army on earth. There was historic reason for this, and part of it involved the horse. Southerners grew up riding elegantly atop their mounts. Northerners were more likely to be riding behind them in a wagon as they plodded to and from the factory. Southern horses could fight. Northern horses could pull machinery. It was the industrialized North against the agrarian South all over again.

As General Taylor had pointed out, horses were more celebrated in the South. Riding was more of a tradition and horsemanship more of an art. And behind every good horse, there usually stood a good man. None was better than James Ewell Brown Stuart.

In the hands of Jeb Stuart, a thousand horses were less of a cavalry than a symphony. For the first half of the war, no one could touch him. It was only at Brandy Station, Virginia, in the early summer of 1863 that his horses suffered their first defeat—defeat being relative; Stuart still held the field at day's end, but his horsemen had been surprised twice and had not downright throttled the enemy as was customary, so the Southern press was not in a charitable mood.

Expectations for Stuart were that high. Few in military history have been so dominant in their disciplines as Stuart was with his mounts. It took the Federals two years and an untold number of lives to catch up.

---

[1] After the subsequent Battle of Antietam, McClellan excused his lack of a follow-up attack by griping that his horses were "sore-tongued and fatigued," leading Lincoln to ask what the horses might be doing on their own time that had them so fatigued. Lincoln later apologized for the wisecrack.

Noble as they might be, in an acid test, most of history's heroes could never quite live up to their press clippings. But in Jeb Stuart's case, the press clippings could never quite live up to the man. To be certain, the Richmond papers could be over the top at times, but in general the Jeb Stuart as history remembers him was largely spot-on. The enduring image of Stuart from the ground up begins with a pair of glistening, knee-length boots of such enormity that they could conceivably have been worn by a man twice his size. Stuart's sash was yellow, his cape lined with red. A flower might smile from his lapel. Then there was that cinnamon beard, an organism unto itself that spilled down his chest like a furry waterfall and seemed all out of proportion to the exposed portion of Stuart's face. His men would watch the fibers of his beard for the telltale ripples that told them that, somewhere in there, Stuart was smiling. Topping off this human work of abstract art was the traditional caviler's hat, the brim rolled up on one side and an ostrich plume rippling in the breeze.

Swashbuckling, fun-loving, feared—the mere rumor of Stuart in the vicinity could cause the Federals to call off an attack. At West Point, he had been a good student and a bad boy, graduating thirteenth in his class, but with, count 'em, 129 behavior-related demerits. Stuart family lore mildly protests the class rank; the story goes that he sloughed off his academics down the home stretch for fear that his good grades would land him a stale job building bridges with the other brainy and boring engineers. (The demerits for conduct, by contrast, appear not to be an issue.)

An outsized personality to be sure, Stuart's clear voice and ringing laugh punctuated an air of dash and gallantry, where fighting and flirting were the order of the day, and were on occasion barely separable. When the Confederates chased the Federals out of Northern Virginia in the late summer of 1862 and crossed the Potomac into Maryland, Stuart decided his men deserved a party. On a walk the evening of September 8 near Urbana, he discovered the Landon House, a conveniently unoccupied mansion with an ample ballroom. His officers were tasked with decorating the property with a forest-fire's

J.E.B. Stuart rode hard and played hard. Once he excused himself from a ball and went out to shoot some Yankees before returning to the dance. (Courtesy National Archives)

worth of candles and sprays of roses. All the residents of Urbana were invited (except for the men) and music and laughter echoed through the night of September 9, until a Union cavalry unit showed up uninvited. Stuart's men excused themselves, hopped on their horses, whipped the Yankees, and returned to the ball, barely missing a dance. Stuart's "Sabers and Roses" ball is celebrated in Frederick to this day.

Stuart's exploits on the battlefield are just as memorable, but perhaps the action that most typifies the man was a simple reconnaissance assignment that Stuart—simple not being his forte—turned into an epic ride around the Union army and an epic embarrassment to Gen. George McClellan.

In the spring of 1862, McClellan had shipped his army down the Chesapeake Bay and was driving up the James River toward Richmond. Robert E. Lee, newly installed as commander of the Confederate eastern army had his back solidly against Richmond's outskirts. Lee had a plan, but for it to work he needed to know the status of McClellan's right flank. Was it solidly anchored in a defensible position, or was it ripe for the picking? Lee called on the man who served as his "eyes and ears" but who was also could be something of a worry left to his own devices. Lee solemnly outlined to Stuart his need for intelligence behind enemy lines. Then, perhaps seeing those auburn whiskers giving away a grin, Lee turned the rest of his orders into a general "what not to do" list that much resembled a father's instructions upon giving his son the keys to the family car. The "greatest caution" must be exercised; he was to "return as soon" as the job was done; he was "not to hazard unnecessarily"; he was "not to attempt" any craziness.

Stuart's grin grew wider. Lee's sigh grew deeper. He tried again:

*Remember that one of the chief objectives of your ex-
pedition is to gain intelligence for the guidance of future
movements . . . Should you find the enemy moving to his
right, or is so strongly posted as to make your expedition
inopportune, you will . . .*

If Stuart were even still listening at this point, he was way
past "inopportune" and was well on his way to "just plain
nuts." He chose 1,200 good riders and selected officers whom
he awakened at two in the morning with the charge that "in
ten minutes every man must be in his saddle." In seven hours
his troop had ridden north to the Union's right flank near the
town of Hanover Court House, where Patrick Henry had once
been a rabble-rouser by day and a bartender by night. Here the
first Union troops were spotted in a numbers and positions
indicating that they were indeed vulnerable to Lee's attack.

Stuart's mission was accomplished. And it was just beginning.

Stuart routed a small band of 150 Federal cavalry, and his
presence was no longer a secret, or it shouldn't have been. But
for the Union, wrote Burke Davis, "a three-day nightmare of
confusion and fumbling had just begun." Stuart turned his
men to the east and began running into, and scattering, Union
horsemen who failed to set off a greater alarm because they appeared not to be believing what they were seeing. "Nothing to
worry about," read one dispatch.

In fact, there was. Federal attempts to shoo away what they
believed were a few stray Confederates were overwhelmed by
Stuart's sizable column, which swallowed up Federal prisoners,
horses, and mules by the dozen. Supply wagons were raided of
their contents and burned. One of these wagons had a load of
Champagne and cigars destined for a Union general, and—it

was poetic justice for Stuart, perhaps—officers soon had more trouble from their own men as they did the Federals, as they rode through the ranks trying too keep too many corks from being prematurely popped.

If anything, riding around an army is trickier than it sounds, because at some point it becomes necessary to ride through the army, or at least the umbilical cord of supply trains and communication lines that connect the army to friendly confines back home. Stuart shattered these lines, cutting telegraph wires and burning freight cars filled with hay and moored barges shipping supplies to McClellan. In the middle of administering mayhem, Stuart's men were startled by a train whistle, and watched as a locomotive pulling flatcars loaded with Federal troops rambled into sight. Seeing the Rebels, the engineer applied full throttle (and got shot for his trouble) and away sped the train, as one of the war's more surreal battles ensued— Stuart's men on horseback exchanging fire with Union troops on rail cars. Stuart called to the rear for one of the few artillery pieces he'd brought along, but the gun was hopelessly sunken up to its axle in mud. All the whipping and profanity that the teamsters could muster had no effect. Finally, desperate men employed desperate measures. A pilfered keg of whiskey was balanced on the gun, with notice that anyone who could pull it free got the booze. A company of German didn't have to be told twice before wading into mud to their waists and lifting the weapon to solid ground.

Virginians had gotten wind of the raid even if the Union hadn't and lined the country road to hug and hold men from their families whom they hadn't seen since the beginning of the war. For many, it was a poignant march, since they had now passed the point of no return. Federal troops were finally starting to give chase; it was not hard, for all they had to do was follow the trail of flames and billowing smoke. For the Federal Keystone Cops, it was still a challenge. At one point, the solitary figure of John Mosby was approached by Federal cavalry. Knowing his horse was exhausted, Mosby, wrote Emory Thomas, "resorted to a desperate bluff. He drew his saber, turned in his saddle and waved imaginary followers forward." The Federal horsemen pulled up short.

Rumor and horror stories spread through the Union ranks. *Something* was out there. They didn't know what. They heard it might be Stuart. They hoped it wasn't. Through a long night, union pickets with nerves strung tight as piano wires strained their ears for any sound and shot at the slightest rustle in the hedges. It was, recalled one Union sentry, "a bad night for cows."

Still, Confederate cavalry riders thought their chances were no better than one in ten—but they followed on with glee, having, one wrote, "implicit confidence and unquestioning trust" in their leader. It was, said Mosby, a "carnival of fun" as they burned and pillaged, and overran the portable grocery stores that followed the armies around. It was the ultimate boys' night out. By the following evening, the raiders were swilling stolen wine and gorging on figs, beef tongue, pickles, cakes, sausages, jam, ketchup, and whatever else the sutlers (suppliers of victuals to the military) might have been peddling.

It was the high point of the ride. The rest was worry and work. With obviously no time to sleep, the men napped in their saddles, including Stuart himself, who had to be steadied by an officer to keep him from falling off his horse. The critical point arrived at what was supposed to be a manageable ford across the Chickahominy, but turned out to be an impassable torrent of floodwater. Figuring the jig was up, many men simply slid off their mounts and collapsed in the grass, too tired to care. The Union cavalry were indeed in pursuit, but with seemingly little urgency. An enduring intrigue is the behavior of the man giving chase, Gen. George Cooke, who had the added title of father-in-law of Jeb Stuart.

The engineers, whose career path Stuart had once shunned, were now of considerable use. Pressed into action, they were able to cobble a makeshift bridge balanced on the abutments of a burned bridge, allowing Stuart's men to cross into relative safety just as the first Union trooper appeared on the river's north side. He fired a single shot. Like everything else thrown at Stuart over the past thirty-six hours, it was ineffective.

In Richmond, the newspapers could not be contained. Magnificent. Brilliant. Unparalleled, they gushed. Columns were filled with explosive accounts of the ride, all of them marvelous, none of them true, a soldier recounted. Confederates reckoned that, while losing only one man, they had captured a couple of hundred Yankees, burned as many wagons, and cost the Union upwards of $2 million in property damage. McClellan, no surprise, downplayed the raid. Just some routine troublemakers who "fired into a train" and "destroyed some wagons." McClellan said he sent in some infantry, which "ran them off."

All of this was inaccurate. But the truth would have been too embarrassing.

CHAPTER 12

An Original, American Piece of Work

To some, Union Maj. Gen. Daniel Sickles almost lost the Battle of Gettysburg single-handedly, and as such all but cost the North the Civil War. Any true fan of Dan Sickles, however, is liable to shrug apathetically at this event, it being, all told, only about the fifth or sixth most interesting thing to happen to the man during the course of his eventful life.

Number one on the list? Hard to say. Maybe it was when he murdered the son of Francis Scott Key. Might have been the time he introduced a whore to English royalty. Could have been his tryst with the beefy but insatiable ex-queen Isabella II, or the fact that he allowed himself to be bilked out of so much of the money he had stolen. He spent some time at Tammany Hall, but the inmates of that particular asylum appeared to be too honest for him. So he moved on to Congress and immediately drank it under the table.

Dan Sickles didn't know the first blessed thing about the military, which explains why by the summer of 1863 he was a general in charge of his own 10,000-man corps in the army of the Potomac. He is, perhaps, best understood in the parlance of Gilbert and Sullivan's ditty about a street urchin who got his start wiping the grime off of the doorknob at a law office: *I polished up the handle so carefully/That now I am the ruler of the Queen's Navy.*

After its army spent a wretched winter on the Rappahannock in 1862–63, the North placed its chips on "Fighting Joe" Hooker, a general of some ability who didn't always pick his officers and drinking buddies—who invariably were one and the same—well. The bacteria that was Dan Sickles blossomed in Hooker's inner petrie dish of wine, women, and song, and Sickles also carefully wormed his way into President Abraham Lincoln's circles, where his uncouth antics occasionally amused the president, and had mixed, but generally favorable, results with the president's wife.

Hooker probably deserved better than he got in Chancellorsville, the first major battle under his command. Unlike McClellan, Hooker had no qualms about taking action. He led his army on an ambitious flanking maneuver, only to get outflanked himself at least partly because Sickles misread the movement of Stonewall Jackson's men as a retreat instead of an attack. As evening approached, Jackson was treated to the sound of gunfire interspersed with momentous cheers that signaled another field taken by the South. Capt. Richard Eggleston Wilbourn, Jackson's signal officer, estimated the Yanks were being driven back at the rather amazing rate of two miles an hour.

At Chancellorsville, Sickles is generally credited with fighting well, but stupidly. Notably, he launched a "midnight attack" that failed because—in the one circumstance Sickles could hardly have been expected to foresee—it was dark. No matter. Sickles established what would become a pattern by blaming others for messes of his own making, or taking credit for quelling crises that he himself caused, even though they usually had to be quelled by someone else.

One tragedy of Dan Sickles—there are many—is that he possessed the one quality no other Union commander seemed to have at the time: aggressiveness. At Chancellorsville, Sickles wanted to advance, but was pulled back by Hooker, a sore point that would come into play later in the summer.

If Hooker had been undermined by his old drinking buddy's analysis, the commander seemed more perturbed by his bosses. In a snit that Washington had failed to recognize his genius following the defeat, he haughtily tendered his resignation, and seemed stunned when Lincoln accepted it. Lincoln's choice to replace Hooker was a turtle-eyed general named George Meade, who was pretty much the opposite of Sickles in every possible way—sober, a professional soldier, level-headed, apolitical—the two were bound to clash.

Dan Sickles had arrived at this point by allegedly living a life that made war seem almost serene by comparison, as summarized in a gripping biography, *Sickles at Gettysburg*, by James Hessler. The son of wealthy parents, Sickles was sent to grow up in a home that included an infant girl named Teresa who would one day become his wife, but not before Sickles had carried on an affair with her mother. By his late teens he had been charged with theft, which began a lifelong career of filching money and property in ways that were sometimes interesting, sometimes not. Nor did his endeavors in Democratic politics at Tammany Hall—vote-fixing, ballot-tampering, financial funny business and the occasional brawl—stand out in the grand scheme of his life. Sickles spent time as a state assemblyman and as a kept man, the keeper being a prostitute and/or madam named Fanny, who saw to it that Sickles always had plenty of cash on hand.

Sickles, in turn, exchanged Fanny's talents for political favors in Albany. The arrangement worked well enough until Sickles got the aforementioned female infant, now a teen, pregnant, at which point Fanny showed up with a riding crop and beat the living daylights out of Dan in public. If there was a coolness between them after that it wasn't lasting, as Dan got a job in the Buchanan administration and took Fanny to England—never mind that he had subsequently married Teresa—where she made quite the splash with the royals, but not in a good way. Dan and Teresa went on to have a daughter who died an alcoholic after Dan turned his back on her as an adult. Meanwhile, Sickles rode Tammany to Congress and moved with Teresa to Washington where his lifestyle continued to exceed his salary and his bedrooms continued to exceed his wife's. Fed up, perhaps, she took a lover of her own, Philip Barton Key, son of the *Star Spangled Banner*'s writer. Key and Sickles were friends until the affair became public, and which point Sickles shot Key to death in the street and extracted a lengthy mea culpa, in writing, from Teresa. Ever the slippery scoundrel, Sickles was acquitted after filing the nation's first defense of temporary insanity and seeing to it (probably) that poor Teresa's "confession" was printed in newspapers nationwide.

The public blamed Teresa, who was sent back to the Northeast in exile, and it only later blamed Dan when he apparently forgave her and moved back in. It was this disgrace that finally caught up with Sickles and drove him out of Congress and into infamy at Gettysburg.

Despite an early drubbing on the first day of that history-changing battle, Gen. George Meade maneuvered the army into a respectable, defensive position going into day two. The line has famously been described as a fishhook, curled around a hilltop to the north, then extending straight to the south along a slight ridge. But this line had a wart on it, and that wart was Dan Sickles, who against orders moved his corps a half-mile or more forward of the main defense to form a bump that in military terms is called a salient. Not having attended military school, Sickles may not have been up on his definitions, nor may he have known that salients are often undesirable because the men are exposed on three sides instead of just one.

As Sickles's men grandly reformed their lines further toward enemy territory, it was hard for a novice not to be impressed with the show of waving flags and beating drums and the glint of polished brass and steel. But real military men knew what would happen. Winfield Hancock stonily watched the soldiers push into no-man's-land before dryly remarking, "They'll be back." And so they were. At a much faster rate than they had been dispatched. Anyone who was anywhere near Dan Sickles at that point in time was about to pay an awful price.

Technically, Sickles had a point in thinking that better, slightly higher ground was to be had ahead of the main line. But the bigger the bubble the thinner the gum, and Sickles's salient popped in several places, with gaps that the Rebels could easily exploit.

Confederate Gen. James Longstreet attacked with ferocity, cutting down Union soldiers "like blades of grass before the scythe," as they said after just about every battle back then, and eventually driving them from positions that are now classically known in Gettysburg history as the Peach Orchard and the Wheatfield. There is a line of thinking—certainly Sickles himself perpetuated it—that the rogue general's blunder was fortuitous for the North in the sense that Lee's troops spent a terrible amount of energy capturing a position that turned out not to be all that valuable, and in the process the Confederate commander was forced into a series of unfortunate moves, culminating with Pickett's disastrous charge into the Yankee center. Sickles would also claim for the rest of his life that his pushing of the envelope forced Meade to engage the enemy rather than retreat. So any fool could see that the real hero of Gettysburg was one Daniel Sickles.

Luckily, more or less, for Sickles, the Confederates weren't having their best day either, tactically speaking. But all that meant is that the rout didn't happen quite as soon as it probably should have. Again, much of Sickles's corps fought well for a while, but even the Spartans at Thermopylae couldn't have overcome the bad position they had been placed in by their commander. Their ranks shredded, the Federals made their way to the rear with considerable interest, to the area where Sickles was headquartered. Discretion being the better part of valor, the general was on his way out too, when a bounding Rebel cannonball pulverized his right leg. History almost lost Dan Sickles at that point, but even this episode worked out largely in his favor.

One, the catastrophic injury might have saved him from a court martial for insubordination. And although there's little that's romantic about losing a leg, Sickles's exit from the battlefield in a horse-drawn ambulance only added to his lore. ". . .[T]he loss of one of his legs in battle helped keep the heroic side of his character in the public mind," states his obit in the *New York Times*. And at some point, someone jammed a lit cigar between his lips, giving the impression that the grievously wounded general was calm, cool, and collected (drugged to the gills might have been more like it) even in the face of such a momentous calamity. There's a chance, a fairly good chance even, that this never happened. But someone said it did, and the story was off to the races. Sickles himself related the story of course, but only after he had been told about it by someone who claimed to have "been there."

Dan Sickles, seated, obviously, never fought again after losing a leg at Gettysburg, although the wound in some ways was really the beginning of his military career. Mark Twain remarked that Sickles seemed to value the missing leg over the one he had left. (Courtesy National Archives)

For the remainder of his life, Sickles made hay out of his missing leg, which, Mark Twain observed, he appeared to value above the one he had left. For Sickles, said Hessler, it wasn't an amputation as much as it was a "career move." The catastrophic injury gave Sickles street cred with veterans, particularly among his embattled 3rd Corps, most of which would have followed him through hell.

. Finally, the wound gave the naughty general one last advantage. Sickles was transported back to Washington to recuperate, and because of this he got to tell his version of the battle to Lincoln before Meade filed his official report. The president visited a recuperating Sickles, and while their conversation is unrecorded, there is little in Sickles's life to suggest that he would be a man to downplay his own heroism while giving due credit to those who actually deserved it.

Lincoln and Sickles, Honest Abe and Dishonest Dan, were a curious pair. At the outbreak of the war, Lincoln the Republican needed, politically speaking, all the pro-war, pro-Union Democrats he could get his hands on, and in this regard Sickles was a perfect fit. This also explained his rapid rise to the position of general, despite his paucity of military experience. Sickles, whose greatest asset was the sensitivity of his political antenna, knew Lincoln needed him and played on his relative value to the point where he would become something of a fixture at White House dinners—where he was not shy about telling all present that it was he who had pulled victory at Gettysburg out of the defeated jaws of Meade. The president, it appears, listened politely but didn't buy a word of it. Once his wound had healed, Sickles begged Lincoln to return him to command of his beloved 3rd Corps, but the president always seemed to have some other, "more important" errand for

Sickles to run, which usually involved sending Sickles to lands foreign and domestic that kept hundreds if not thousands of miles between Dan Sickles and any chance to order more men to slaughter. At war's end, Sickles found himself tasked to South America.

In between these sojourns, Sickles pounded away at his lifelong theme: He had been right, Meade had been wrong. He appeared before Congress and told Meade's enemies (Republicans distrusted the degree to which the hearts of West Pointers such as Meade were in the fight) what they wanted to hear. When cornered by the facts, Sickles's version of the "truth" would pop up somewhere else, usually parroted by his lackeys, but sometimes in more original formats with results that were equal parts hilarious and pathetic.

At one of his lower points on the credibility scale, a mysterious and anonymous scribe who dubbed himself "Historicus" began writing for a New York City paper on the grounds that he was an eyewitness to the Battle of Gettysburg and needed to clear the air about what had transpired on the second day of the battle, lest history be forever deceived. Historicus's story was a carbon of Sickles's, with a few surplus laurels thrown in that the general might have been too shy to award himself up front, had he been signing his own name to the piece.

With the cessation of hostilities, Sickles got back to his role as America's scoundrel laureate, chasing women and civil service appointments with equal relish. He was appointed to head up the South Carolina district during Reconstruction and almost wound up rekindling the war. But this only won him a bigger and better assignment as ambassador of Spain in 1869, where he catted around in the royal court, took up with deposed queen Isabella II, and wound up marrying the daughter of a Spanish Councillor of State, with whom he had two children before washing his hands of the lot of them and jumping ship back to New York. If he hadn't exactly started the Spanish-American War, his appalling Ugly American manners and obsession with Cuba at least laid a plausible foundation.

Once home, Dan Sickles quickly got back to the never-ending task of promoting Dan Sickles. This was important, since the grownups in the military were always bad-mouthing his performance at Gettysburg and Sickles felt the need to try to stay one step ahead. He was good at it, getting himself appointed to the New York Monument Commission—he wanted nothing so much as a statue to himself at Gettysburg—as well as sitting in on veterans groups and anniversary celebrations. These were the perfect platforms for perpetuating his story, and his audiences of veterans were always more than ready to offer him a hero's welcome (even if the books of the organizations that Sickles directed usually reflected, sooner or later, large chunks of missing cash). An aging Sickles would always show up late, and make a show of dragging himself—missing leg at the fore—down the main aisle to the stage where he was to speak. Nor did he mind being at the center of attention, even when he wasn't. Once, at the funeral of a fellow officer, Sickles settled himself at a point in the viewing room where he was sure to draw more attention than the corpse.

This life of charades and lies tinged with perpetual scandal could only lead to one thing: Sickles was reelected to Congress, where, to his credit, he introduced legislation that established the Gettysburg National Battlefield and championed its (and his, of course) place in history.

A favored line of Sickles's was that he had never before spoken about the events of Gettysburg, but attacks on his honor made it necessary now. In the end, however, Sickles spoke "for the first time" about Gettysburg so many times that he overplayed his hand. That afternoon in early July so many years ago began to define and dominate his existence. A random question on an unrelated topic could somehow be twisted by Sickles into an avenue for defending his behavior at Gettysburg while attacking Meade's.

Mark Twain's experience with Sickles had been typical, although Twain was better armed than most to put the experience into words. As fate would have it, Twain wound up living across the street from Sickles in New York, but the two famous men never visited ("he is too old, I am too lazy," Twain explained) until an acquaintance of both virtually dragged the great writer across the street. Twain endured what he could of Sickles's "monotonous talk—it was about himself, is always about himself." Yet Twain seemed bemused in a melancholy sort of way by the old man, whom he called "winningly childlike."

Dan Sickles, documented murderer, liar, thief, cheater, philanderer, two-timer, and insubordinate, lived long enough to witness in person the fiftieth anniversary of the Battle of Gettysburg. No other corps commander on either side held out that long. Sickles almost had to in the cosmic scheme of things, although this milestone came with a price. Well into his nineties, his body and mind were shot. Once a wealthy man, he was now a pauper and only escaped arrest for his debts thanks to the charity of his estranged family. He was dead within a year of the reunion, and he went to his grave with the bitter knowledge that—despite his best attempts to spin history in his favor—no statue of himself stared out onto the scene of his most famous act. Yet for a couple of days in

July, 1913, Sickles was once again surrounded by the men he cherished, the men of the 3rd Corps whose record, like Sickles's, had become the subject of so much derision. One last time they joined together in laughter and tears and hugs and stories, lubricated with copious quantities of liquor. Sickles's mind came and went, but he knew he was among friends; he knew he was a great leader of men, and he knew that he was loved.

At Gettysburg today, there is a grand monument out in the fields, near the site of the 3rd Corps's encounter with Longstreet, a monument that is a tribute to Sickles's New York Excelsior Brigade. But something, on examination, is obviously missing. Five columns encircle a pedestal, but the pedestal is empty. The explanation of this situation isn't historically solid, but it's good. At one time a bust of Dan Sickles was supposedly to have been proudly placed at the monument's center, a reminder to future generations of the general's important service to his country. When it came time to hire a sculptor to chisel the statue, however, the members of the New York Monument Commission were shocked to discover that there was no money left in the agency's accounts to pay for the project. The money for the statue of Dan Sickles had been stolen—by former monument committee chairman Dan Sickles.

CHAPTER 13

Spare Time

War was hell, but it had its moments. Robert E. Lee famously commented that it was a good thing war was so bloody, otherwise it would be too much fun. Frequent are the descriptions of idle brigades during battle whose soldiers were agitating to get into the fray. At Appomattox, Maj. Gen. Joshua Chamberlain reported that dedicated scrapper Phil Sheridan seemed rather gloomy over Lee's surrender. After the truce had been declared, gunfire erupted on a far flank. Sheridan was about to send an urgent message to his men to cease the slaughter when he was overcome by nostalgia. "Aw hell," he said, reconsidering. "Let'em fight."

For the boys, war was at first a new experience. But then, just about anything that didn't involve plowing fields and pulling stumps would have been a new experience. Some had never shot a gun, nor had they traveled more than a few miles beyond their own property. More than a few had never seen a naked lady.

Many men would die needlessly because the raw recruits didn't have the faintest clue how to cook a pot of beans.

All of that was about to change.

And while war might have been hell, the alternative was frequently worse. To the question of what the men did in their spare time, the answer is a grisly surprise: They died. By the hundreds of thousands, they died. Incredible as it might seem, fighting was statistically much safer than sitting around in a cold, wet camp or foul prison with nothing to drink but a muddy swill of water and urine. As unconscionably bloody as Civil War battlefields could be, soldiers faced only a little better (or worse) than one chance in ten of being hit. (Don't tell this, however, to the 26th North Carolina, which lost 588 of 800 men on the first day of Gettysburg; after a day of rest, those who escaped unharmed or weren't hurt too badly were ordered to the center of the battlefield and told to report to a man by the name of Pickett.)

The Union lost 110,000 men to battlefield deaths; more than twice that number died of disease or accidents. The South lost 94,000 in battle, but 164,000 died of other causes. Some of those "other causes" included colorful episodes of drownings, equipment malfunction, and even murder. The Union lost 300 men to sunstroke and 400 to suicide. But most fatalities were caused by disease, treated, more often than not, with medieval concoctions such as mercury that only made things worse.

In the dead of winter, 1861–62—months before the South's first major foray into Maryland—Stonewall Jackson was itching to invade the border state with a small force based in what is now Berkeley Springs, West Virginia. Across the Potomac River in the town of Hancock was an even smaller Federal force determined to offer what resistance it could. As John H. Nelson conveys in his meticulously researched booklet *Bombard and Be Damned*, nothing much happened here, militarily speaking. Jackson's emissary crossed the river to demand Hancock's surrender under pain of being shelled. An apathetic Union commander told him to feel free to begin the bombardment whenever he wished, since most of the people in town were Southern sympathizers anyway.

Outside of a few shells lobbed back and forth, the B&O railroad and a couple of churches took the worst of it. But a lot happened at Hancock in terms of understanding the threats faced by soldiers in camp. While battlefield casualties were scarce, disease was a more frequent visitor. Included in Nelson's notes is a list of men who died, and the cause of death. An abridged survey would include: Frank Vananken, typhoid; Elijah Leggett, typhoid; Horace Lane, typhoid; James Barrett, drowned while on guard duty; Amos Wenrich, drowned after slipping on the ice when he was crossing the C&O canal to get a cup of coffee; Owen Bullard, gastritis; Andrew Ward, measles; Joseph Austin, chronic diarrhea; Franklin Ward, typhoid; Amos Thompson, accidentally shot; George Collins, exposure; Henry Reid, malignant sore throat; and so on.

Camp conditions were far more worrisome to the soldiers than the enemy, wrote the 19th New York regimental historian: "The mortality in the 19th at this place was great. The village was one execrable mudhole, and what with fatigue and picket duties, colds and fevers began to abound. The unconquerable disposition of the soldiers to shut themselves up close in their quarters without ventilation made the evil a hundredfold worse." Sensing that fresh air would help, doctors knocked out windows to "purify the air," but the freezing soldiers patched them up as soon as the physician left. Fires helped take the edge off the chill, but weren't always allowed because they could give away a regiment's position. That was a bad proposition during an Arctic snap in which the Potomac froze six inches deep in a single night and the temperature dipped to 16 below. On the evening of Hancock's bombardment, both sides were literally shooting in the dark, until Jackson called it off at 10 PM. War in these conditions, reported Confederate gunner George Neese, just wasn't any fun:

> *The snow is four inches deep and the night is very unfavorable for an outdoor performance; and to add to the disagreeableness of the situation, an icy breeze is creeping over the frozen hills and feels like a breath from the North Pole. At last about two hours after midnight, an order came around permitting us to make fires, and I never saw fences disappear so fast.*

Snow wasn't always the worst element soldiers faced. That honor would probably go to mud. Spring thaws and rains made for some of the most miserable conditions an army could (or couldn't) travel through. Despite some early stabs at macadam on the National Pike in Maryland and elsewhere, most rural roads were unpaved and barely improved. That could be inconvenient enough for one horse or wagon, but men and horses by the tens of thousands pulling ton after ton of cannon and supplies turned dirt pathways into murderous ribbons of muck that seemed to suck boot, wagon wheel, and hoof toward the center of the earth. On their way to Berkeley Springs, Jackson's men had settled uncomfortably at a place called Unger that was known to the soldiers as "Camp Mud."

Simple jaunts could turn into arduous, day-long treks. In battle, needed guns frequently were not forthcoming because they were paralyzed by goo; there were times when mud affected the outcome of a scrap more than the soldiers did. And sometimes mud prevented the battle from beginning at all. That happened in January of 1863, when the hapless Union Gen. Ambrose Burnside boldly determined that he would atone for his failure at Antietam; that he would atone for his failure at Fredericksburg; that he would atone for—well, atone for just about every military action he'd been involved in up to that point.

A month earlier, Burnside had made a wreck of the Federal army at Fredericksburg—a slaughter so bad it had nearly brought even the enemy to tears. Burnside now declared the arrival of "a great and auspicious moment" that would allow him to "strike a great and mortal blow" to the rebellion. His plan was to sneak up the bank of the Rappahannock, cross the river on pontoon bridges, and take Lee's unprotected left flank by surprise. The plan might have been a good one, but no one will ever know because almost immediately it devolved into a horrid failure, even by Ambrose's storied standards. A brief winter warm-up and ensuing rains turned the Virginia countryside into one big wallow that swallowed Burnside's soldiers and horses up to the knees. Entire corps became delayed and confused and marched into each other's paths. The army's pontoon boats were pulled by one, then two, then three teams of mules and horses, ultimately to no avail. Men joined in on the tugging—up to 150 ropes were secured to each pontoon wagon, and the order given to heave to. One officer recounted, "They would founder through the mire for a few feet—the gang of Lilliputians with their huge-ribbed Gulliver—and then give up breathless." One New York regiment was able to move only a mile and a half in a day. Burnside, bless his heart, was running up and down the lines in a near panic, doing everything he could to salvage the operation short of tugging on the ropes himself. The general and his horse became a mud-lacquered allegory of despair, as his dream of redemption and glory turned into yet another horrific blunder. A heartbreaking account by historian Ernest B. Furguson, in his book *Chancellorsville 1863*, quotes a New York surgeon who summed up Burnside's pathetic situation: "We could but think that the soldier on foot, arm oppressed with the weight of knapsack, haversack and gun, bore an easy load compared with that of the commander of the army, who now saw departing his hopes of redeeming the prestige he had lost at Fredericksburg."

By this time, the surprise had gone out of his attack of course, but it still might have succeeded if only because Confederates on the opposite bank of the river were paralyzed with laughter at the North's predicament. They elevated their merriment by painting large billboards with arrows advising THIS WAY TO RICHMOND and offering to help the Yanks place their pontoons, since they were making such poor work of it themselves.

Even as he was losing his mission and the hearts of his men, Burnside wouldn't give up. In order to boost morale, he ordered the distribution of a healthy ration of whiskey. Strangely, this didn't help. One officer reported "An indescribable chaos of pontoons, wagons, and artillery encumbered the road down to the river. Horses and mules dropped down dead, exhausted with the effort to move their loads through the hideous medium. One hundred and fifty dead animals, many of them buried in the liquid muck, were counted in the course of a mornings ride." Burnside and his army finally gave up and slogged back to a camp they had all hoped never to see again.

In fact, this encampment, known that winter as "Camp Misery," was one of the reasons Burnside felt the need to move his men in the first place. As with Hancock, this was a cold, damp incubator of disease, only on a much larger scale. So happy had some men been to leave that they burned their huts—now they returned to nothing. It was almost more than they could bear.

In one sense, at least for the men, the Civil War amounted to a handful of epic battles flanked by days, weeks, months, and years of mind-numbing inactivity. Camp life could be horribly dull. If not on a campaign, the soldier's day began at five or six in the morning, and revolved around a series of monotonous practices.

An oft-quoted Pennsylvania recruit summed it up: "The first thing in the morning is drill, then drill, then drill again. Then drill, drill, a little more drill. Then drill and lastly drill. Between drills we drill and sometimes stop to eat a little and have a roll call." Drilling was not popular and its appeal decreased with each passing year. A petrified old vet wrote, or tried to, "Brigade drill and review today i dont know what will cum tomoror and dont cair one god dam sir."

In the summer soldiers generally slept in two-man shelters (on the march, each man carried half a tent and the sides were buttoned together in camp). Many soldiers felt these canvas contrivances were little better than "dog houses," and perhaps this sobriquet was a forebearer of the term "pup tent". In winter, such as at Camp Misery, quarters were built along organized streets and constructed of logs, much like miniature frontier cabins. They were equipped with stoves and furniture that were as elaborate as the soldiers desired. Some gave their crude homes names such as "The Astor House."

Soldiers passed the time in a variety of ways. Gambling was important, and so was religion. The prevalence of the two was directly proportional to the immanency of battle. The roads to major battlefields were often littered with dice and cards, tossed aside by those with a heightened interest in salvation.

Perhaps the best virtue-versus-vice story, although also perhaps apocryphal, involved one soldier with a Bible in his breast pocket fighting alongside a man who, instead of the holy book, was carrying a pack of cards. Both men were struck in the same spot, but the bullet bounced off the pious man's Bible and burrowed into his heart and killed him. The bullet that struck the gambler pierced fifty-one cards but was stopped by the last one, the ace of spades. Soldiers wrote poetry and plays that they acted out for the men. Music was always popular. They fished in the streams and swam in the rivers—it would not have been particularly noteworthy to see Yankees and Rebels swimming in the same hole. They chased greased pigs, ran races, engaged in shooting matches. Baseball was popular, as were reading, playing cards, hunting, snaring rabbits, and writing letters.

In one sense, perhaps, the men got a better education than they would have received at home, since so much idle time was taken up by reading and writing—skills they would not have had time to hone had they been home. Bell Irvin Wiley published fascinating books on camp life ferreted out of more than 30,000 soldiers' letters home. (These letters are priceless, among other things, for their homespun similes, including "It was short and sweet, like a roasted maggot," and "These Southerners are poorer than skim piss.")

Yet for all the terrors of war, and of waiting around for war, some soldiers clearly thought the Civil War was a blast. "Never enjoyed anything in the world as I do this life," wrote a kid from Illinois. For some in 1860, getting shot at, frozen, half starved, and marched to the point of exhaustion still might have represented a marginal improvement over their current home life up to that point. Some had never seen underwear, nor had any idea of what to do with it. A standing prank among the veterans was to tell the raw recruit that there was a special type of uniform to be worn during dress parades. Pranks were a big deal. When a recruit was stationed as a sentry for the first time, vets would creep out into the bush and rattle around a bit. When the high-strung rookie shouted, "Who goes there?" a voice in the dark would answer "A flock of sheep," or other nonsense.

Soldiers saved their best humor, however, for the food. Army rations were the most important part of the war and the most derided. At least they were in the North; in the South, rations were so scarce that any food was considered good food. Armadillo, raved one Rebel, was "superior to any possum meat I ever eat."

Federals had the luxury of grousing. It was a pity, said one, that Sampson was not in possession of U.S. Army butter, because he could have rubbed his bald head with it and the Philistines wouldn't have touched him.

If men couldn't cry over the quality of the horribly over-brined beef they could at least laugh. One regiment enacted a grand dress procession, complete with a military band, that gave full honors to a barrel of beef and buried it with a somber twenty-one-gun salute out of respect for "its long service to the army."

In camp, men who got along well would break out into "messes" of four to eight and take turns cooking, cleaning, and foraging. If they were lucky, they would have black cooks whose skills in the culinary arts far exceeded those of boys straight off the farm. (Courtesy National Archives)

One Illinois soldier said you could throw the beef up against a tree and it would "quiver and twitch" like a lizard that had been poked with a stick. Another said he suspected the army was feeding mule meat to the troops because their ears had grown three-and-a-half inches since arriving in Annapolis. In the South, this was no laughing matter; a ration of mule went around to the men under siege at Petersburg. Few Confederates were in a position to complain.

Rations could, and were supposed to, include many things, but most reliably for the North they included bread, salt pork, beans, and coffee. The South subsisted primarily on meal and meat that often walked a gray line between bacon and suet. Lee loved it when he could get something as simple and nourishing as a shipment of field peas.

A frequently bent rule was that men were not supposed to steal the edible possessions of private citizens. But hunting was allowed, so hogs were explained away as being "slow deer." One Irishman was reprimanded when an officer caught him with a chicken hanging from his gun. The soldier protested his innocence, saying he had caught the hen laying eggs for the support and comfort of the Rebels and "Aye stopped that act of trayson on the spot, bejesus."

Tragically, the South had plenty of food; the problem was that it so infrequently reached the soldiers. Some of this was attributable to the predictable afflictions of graft, red tape, and inefficient distribution. But there were other problems that included a lack of simple shipping containers. And while the South had plenty of food, it did not have much of the key ingredient needed to preserve that food: salt. Thousands of barrels of food spoiled as it sat on railroad loading docks. Consequently, borderline starvation in the South was frequently an issue. Men were known to scrape up the dirt where the horses had been fed and wash the till at night in hopes of salvaging a few kernels of spilled grain. Certainly there were acute food shortages in the North at times, but as a general thing, Federal troops had enough or knew they soon would. When they didn't, heads would roll.

Our poor friend Burnside lost the faith of his men, but it had less to do with the Mud March than it did his inability to burst the bottlenecks that kept proper rations from reaching Camp Misery. This was the last straw, and Burnside was replaced by a man who, as his name implies, had his own impact on the spare time and society of camp life: Joe Hooker.

Just as Paris Hilton is not the source of the word "hot," Gen. Joe Hooker was not the source of the common nickname for prostitutes. But by the time he was done, the nation (and history) could be excused for thinking he was. He certainly popularized it. On a surprise visit from Lincoln, a flock of these "soiled doves" reportedly scattered from the doorstep of Hooker's headquarters like spooked rabbits. Along with the generals who became his drinking buddies, Hooker cultivated an atmosphere in his tent that drew scathing rebukes from the pious and the God-fearing—it was a combination of barroom and brothel, sniffed one officer. But Hooker alone could hardly be blamed for the prostitution that followed the army like seagulls after a shrimp boat.

At the time of the Civil War, prostitution was legal. In Washington alone, there were 500 brothels—creatively named "Unconditional Surrender," "Headquarters USA," and such—and 5,000 prostitutes. Washington's most famous madam, Mary Ann Hall, died in 1886 having amassed a fortune that today would be worth close to $2 million. Female "followers" of the armies tagged along under the titles of being cooks and cleaners, although in truth they did little of either. Memphis, meanwhile, became known as the Gomorrah of the West and Nashville was home to a famous, soldier-friendly strip known as Smokey Row. The women were routinely chased away, but came right back. This was a problem, because venereal disease would ultimately touch eight percent of the army. One general ordered all prostitutes to board a steamboat and sent them upriver, where the mayors of Louisville, Cincinnati, and so on, were waiting on the docks telling the captain to keep moving. Ultimately the ship's pilot had nowhere to go but back. Nashville's problem was eventually solved when prostitutes were licensed and checked by doctors. Women who were infected were sent to a hospital funded by a fifty-cent tax on hookers. The system worked splendidly.

The sex trade also included racy books and pictures, which were especially popular with farm boys who, raised in the Victorian age, knew nothing of female forms beyond the reams of fabric in which the women of the day liberally upholstered themselves.

Published matter, bawdy or otherwise, might be purchased from the sutlers who, along with rolling barrooms and whorehouses, shadowed the troops like mobile convenience stores, selling tobacco, tinned meats, newspapers, and other knickknacks that soldiers might need. Their prices were legend, and they further aggravated the men by tending to disappear not long after payday, when they discerned the bulk of the soldiers' money had been spent.

And there was no quicker way to spend it than when whiskey was for sale. Commanders had whiskey rations that they could dispense as they saw fit, but beyond that, enlisted men were not allowed to purchase spirits. So frequently was this order violated that an exasperated Confederate Gen. Braxton Bragg reckoned that liquor had gotten more of his men killed than enemy bullets. In the 1860s, drinking heavily and drinking on the job and drinking at all hours of the day was accepted, if not always acceptable. Some figured the war itself was caused by whiskey, fueled as it was by hotheaded and often inebriated politicians, newspaper editors, and public rabble-rousers. Thanks to an alleged Lincoln quip, Gen. Ulysses Grant might be the war's most celebrated whiskey swiller—if excess whiskey contributed to Grant's performance, Lincoln was willing to have a barrel of his brand shipped to all his generals. Indeed, after the war, a number of generals had whiskeys named after them, including Grant, Sheridan, Jackson, and Custer.

From the time a recruit signed up, the bottle would begin to be passed his way, even though daily whiskey rations in the army had ended in 1830. Someone always seemed to have a bottle or a flask, whether in a position of authority or not. Author Gerald Carson (*The Social History of Bourbon*) tells of a young fifer who indignantly poured his first discretionary whiskey ration out on the ground. The next time his commanding officer offered a ration he drank it for the first time; and following that experiment, "when the commanding officer gave out whiskey, I yielded to his better judgment."

If the liquor didn't lead to anything more serious than a fight, officers generally looked the other way. And soldiers got good at hiding it—a Southern story tells of soldiers hollowing out and filling up a watermelon; one Union soldier was caught taking a big, long belt from the barrel of his rifle.

Prevalent as it was among the enlisted men, drinking on the part of the officers might have been even more deadly and consequential. It was not uncommon for troops to be unable to move because their commanders were drunk. Prior to the Battle of Franklin, the South missed a golden chance to ambush the Union army because senior officers were enjoying too much of the Tennessee whiskey they'd been given as gifts.

Near Leesburg, a drunken Confederate officer ordered a group of Yankees, whom he mistook for his own men, to attack a position of his own men that he mistook for the enemy's. The Union men, mistaking this drunkard for a member of their own command, did so—and were slaughtered.

Liquor could cause bizarre behavior, but then the war was bizarre in and of itself, and getting more so. The prevalence of whiskey may have endured, but as the war evolved, camp life changed. Modern weapons required a change in tactics, and armies did less marching and camping and more digging in for the long haul. From these entrenchments they would lob shells at each other whenever they were in the mood. On campaigns, the time in between big battles was relatively safe; with trench warfare death might strike from the sky at any moment of any day. In a sense, death was still random, but it was no longer an anomaly.

If war life had ever been fun, as the young Illinois soldier had once claimed, it was becoming less so. What had caused excitement in the beginning now simply made men numb. Everyone was ready for the end.

CHAPTER 14
A Southern Boy Comes Home

For three and a half years, Capt. Tod Carter of Franklin, Tennessee, dreamed of his father's supper table. He dreamed of his large, loving family and their modest but elegant brick home. He dreamed of warm biscuits, smoky bacon, crocks of fresh butter, and tubs of sweet preserves. This was not unusual; these would have been the dreams of many soldiers. Like many other soldiers too, Tod Carter joined the Confederacy at an age when procurement of a razor would have been an overly optimistic purchase. He would be dead at 24. He served mainly as a quartermaster in the Western Theater throughout the hills, valleys, and rivers of Tennessee and Kentucky, his service steady but unremarkable until, with a rush, a raging flood of events began to take him farther and farther from his father's table. Then, by way of a route, and with a suddenness that no one could have imagined, Carter found himself virtually in his father's front yard, riding a horse named

Rosencrantz, screaming above a blinding fray for men to follow him in an attack on his own home.

It was not the homecoming he had imagined. In the house, his family huddled together in indescribable fear as their half-crazed loved one approached. It was not the homecoming they had imagined either.

Tod Carter might have been just another forgotten soldier killed in the war had the circumstances surrounding his death not been so bizarre. (Courtesy Williamson County Heritage Foundation)

For six months in the latter half of the war, fate treated Tod Carter like a rag doll. He had been captured in the Battle of Missionary Ridge in the late fall of 1863. His tacked-up horse had swum the river and made it back to camp sans Tod, leaving his fellows to assume he'd been killed. Instead, Carter was on a prisoner-of-war train heading north toward a camp on Johnson's Island near Sandusky, Ohio. Word of Carter's true whereabouts eventually reached his family, although not exactly. They wrote letters to him in Ohio, not knowing that he had never arrived; he'd duped his guards by pretending to be asleep, and jumped—with a turbo boost from a seatmate's feet—from the train in Pennsylvania. From there, he traveled down the Ohio and Mississippi rivers and eventually rejoined his regiment in Georgia sometime in the spring of 1864.

All things being equal, Carter should have played out the string of the war uneventfully enough, as the Confederate army of Lt. Gen. John Bell Hood dogged Sherman's march to Atlanta. Gen. William Sherman had just captured the city and had no interest in chasing Hood up and down the Appalachian Mountains. So he headed east; in theory, Hood should have followed.

Instead, the Southern general cooked up the scheme that historian James McPherson famously described as being "scripted in never-never land." Even though he would be outnumbered by 20,000 federal troops, he'd go north through Tennessee and Kentucky to the Ohio River and then turn east to join Lee's army of Northern Virginia. Detractors aside, at this point in the war, there might have been no good choices left for the South. Had he tailed Sherman his army of the Tennessee would have become a construction crew doing little but rebuilding the bridges burned by Union men.

Hood, with Carter in tow somewhere, started on a long march north under less than ideal conditions. The army had been battered by Sherman. Soldiers tied rags to their feet in lieu of shoes. Breakfast, lunch, and dinner consisted of a curious knot of coarse wheat flour and water that had none of the culinary advantages that shortening, milk, baking soda, or salt might have lent. The men imaginatively called them "sinkers." Thoughts of the bounties from the Carter's rich farmland would have certainly grown more intense.

On November 21, Hood crossed the Tennessee River with 40,000 men, and prepared to chase down a retreating federal force under his former West Point classmate Gen. John Schofield. If he could whip Schofield before the Union had a chance to consolidate its western forces, he could pick off its other detachments at random, while opening supply lines to Lee in the east and preventing Federal reinforcements from reaching Grant. It sounded plausible, and it almost worked. Instead, in less than six weeks time, Hood's proud, hardened army would no longer exist as an effective fighting force.

Like chess pieces, the armies of Hood and Schofield played off each other, as the Northerner tried to join friendly troops eighteen miles away in Nashville, while the Southerner tried to keep him from doing it. It made for tense feintings and stare-downs, and one game-changing blunder in which Hood's men failed to obey orders to attack and in so doing failed to smash a column of Yankee sitting ducks as they marched north. On November 29, Schofield and his 29,000 men tiptoed around Hood's men at Spring Hill as they slept, a daring move that would have paid off mightily had not the river behind the small town of Franklin not been too swollen to cross. Schofield looked around for promised pontoons on which to build a bridge. They hadn't arrived. His army, its back to the river, would have to take a stand, and his men began scoping out a defensible position. They settled on a promising height of land with some outbuildings that could be dismantled for breast-works, a hill that was named after its owner—a man by the name of Carter.

As Hood's army awakened to find that Schofield had slipped past, Tod Carter was not among the sleepy men. He had decided that it would have been a shame if the war had passed so closely by his home and he had not been allowed to quickly visit the loved ones he hadn't seen in three and a half years. So the day before, he had been issued a pass, giving him permission to go ahead of the army and see his family. Tod Carter was "filled with ecstasy" that he would "eat breakfast at his father's house in the morning." In a family history, Carter's great-grand-niece Rosalie set the scene:

> At home was his aged father, Fountain Branch Carter, now 67. Here too was his older brother, Col. Moscow Branch Carter, who had been a prisoner of war at home on parole for about a year. Here at home were his four sisters and his beloved sister-in-law. In addition were nine little nieces and nephews, all under 12 years of age. No doubt Tod thought of his father's fireside that November day, and the hams and bacon that always filled the smokehouse, and the good meals the servants prepare in the little kitchen in the yard . . . But most of all he longed to sit once more at his father's breakfast table with all the members of his beloved family.

Some years later, the story goes, a newspaper reporter from Philadelphia was poking around for interesting stories from the bygone war when his wagon driver, an old African-American, halted in front of the Carter House. He told the heartbreaking story of Tod Carter, who, in the dim morning light, after an odyssey of better than three years and thousands of miles, got to within a few feet, *feet*, of his front door that morning, when his eye was caught by a member of his family frantically motioning him *away* from the house. It was awash in sleeping Federals whose hearts were unlikely to be warmed by family reunions.

Carter scurried back to his regiment and his family scurried to the basement, where they had taken the precaution of burying some of their most select hams beneath the floorboards.

Many battles have laid claim to being the bloodiest or the most savage of the war. If the Battle of Franklin was not the most violent, atrocious scrap of the war, it should at least be up for an honorable mention. Battlefield guides ask those with weak stomachs to step back from the group before they begin their shtick, saying the fight was "obscene and vile and there's no way to sugarcoat it."

The Battle of Franklin was a compressed head-on collision fought mostly after dark. It's described as the Pickett's Charge of the west, as Confederates came at the Union defenses with everything they had. The desperation on both sides was palpable and piercing, every last soldier frantic to gain whatever small advantage might be attained.

The fight began at four in the afternoon, and for the next five hours straight, a man died every ten seconds—by 9 PM there were 10,000 casualties in all. Six Confederate generals died. Bodies piled up six and seven deep, at such a height that the freshly killed had no place to fall over, and were discovered after the battle standing dead in their tracks. Historian

Eric Jacobson described the fight as a "medieval slugfest in the dark." Soldiers clawed, scratched, gouged, clubbed, bit, kicked, pulled hair, yanked beards, threw rocks and sticks, and rubbed handfuls of dirt in each others eyes. So close were the lines that the crack of rifle volleys were echoed by the crack of men's bones; soldiers standing in front of cannons were vaporized into clouds of pink mist. On the porch of the Carter house, spent rifles were used as skull-pulverizing clubs. The next day, Moscow Carter grabbed a shovel and a basket and, the story goes, proceeded to scoop up a halfbushel of human brain matter. Even hardened veterans were left stupefied by the brutality that was above and beyond anything they had seen in war.

Some men, charged with adrenaline perhaps, refused to go down. Arthur MacArthur was knocked from his horse by a shot to his shoulder. As he rose, his attacker shot him in the chest and, satisfied with the quality of his work, turned his attention to other matters—only to be run through by the sword of a very much alive MacArthur. The dying man got off one more shot at MacArthur, which hit him in the knee. Still, he somehow survived. But as impressive as his performance might have been, MacArthur was eventually outshone in history by his son, World War II hero General Douglas MacArthur.

The Carter family was joined in the stone basement by some neighbors, and they listened to the roar of battle above. Moscow later recounted that "While the terrible din of the battle lasted it seemed to the adults that they must die of terror if it did not cease, but when there was a lull the suspense of fearful expectation seemed worse than the sound of battle." And out there, somewhere, was young Tod.

As an assistant quartermaster and aide de camp, Tod Carter's duties generally did not involve combat, but he could hardly be held back from participating in the task of liberating his own house from the enemy. Rosalie Carter described the scene:

> It was on the first charge and when nearest the enemy's works that Capt. Tod Carter dashed through the lines on his horse Rosencrantz, with drawn sword, reaching as far as his arm would allow toward the enemy. He was leading the charge [when] his horse was seen to plunge and those near him knew he had been struck. Tod was thrown over his horse's head and when he struck the ground he lay very still. The hour was five o'clock, just as the sun was setting. He had been mortally wounded only about 525 feet southwest of his home, the Carter House.

The family and friends meanwhile huddled in the basement, children cowering at their feet, but otherwise bearing up fairly well. Shortly after midnight, the Carter family discerned that the Federals had retired toward Nashville and it was safe to come out of hiding. But their relief was short-lived. A soldier arrived with word that Tod was still alive but grievously wounded, lying out in the darkness and in need of help. With cautious urgency, the family climbed over the Federal breastworks and out into the smoky field. His father, brother and sisters held a lantern up to face after ghostly face in searched of their loved one.

He was found at last, deliriously calling out his commander's name; the officer's final instructions to Tod had been to refrain from attacking too soon, an order that the overzealous young man had failed to obey. He was taken back to the house and laid out on the floor among the dead and dying enemy. He didn't last long. The bullet that lodged in his brain was donated by the family in 2010 to the Battle of Franklin Trust, where it remains on display in the Carter House, in proximity to where Tod Carter breathed his last, surrounded by his sisters as they whispered, "Brother's come home at last."

Chapter 15
Confederate Hopes Sink

O n Sunday June 19, 1864, the town of Cherbourg on the north coast of France was buzzing as it seldom had before—and probably wouldn't again until the Normandy Invasion. More than 5,000 miles from Richmond, the French fishermen and farmers were about to be treated to front row seats to watch an honest-to-goodness battle in America's Civil War.

No one was going to miss this. Some 15,000 spectators jammed the shorelines to see the epic fight.

It was more a seafaring version of a medieval joust, really, with heavy cannon for lances and European diplomats for damsels, whose hearts were there to be won or lost based on the outcome.

In the spirit of the times, the captain of the CSS *Alabama*, Raphael Semmes, dropped the captain of the USS *Kearsarge*, John Winslow a courteous note explaining the program of events.

Captain Winslow:

Sir—I am undergoing a few repairs here which, I hope,
will not take longer than the morrow. Then I will come out
and fight you a fair and square fight.
      Most respectfully yours,
Captain Semmes

The chivalry wouldn't last.

Much of the Civil War's nautical publicity begins and ends with the *Monitor* and the *Merrimack*, the two ironclads that pinged and doinked each other to a draw off the coast of Virginia. But United States and Confederate naval intrigue truly spanned the globe, from the coast of Brazil to the English Channel to the Arctic Circle.

Men of the USS *Kearsarge* allowed the CSS *Alabama* to do its worst before taking the offensive. In the end, the fight was one-sided, but the *Alabama's* captain later cried foul. (Courtesy National Archives)

The CSS *Alabama* never spent any time in Southern ports, and in her two-year career only caught a glimpse or two of the Confederate coast. Her job was specifically to terrorize Union merchant ships, and she, along with a handful of other cruisers of her class, was quite effective.

Unable to match the shipbuilding prowess of the North, the Confederate's idea of a Navy was a network of gunboats and booby traps to guard its harbors at home, and a fleet of daring pirate ships on the high seas to put pressure on the Federal economy.

Both practices had their moments, good and bad. When the South floated defensive mines (called torpedoes back in the day) in Southern harbors there were indeed effective, but rapidly corroded.

Much of the South's shipping commerce had been more or less put out of business by one of the last great acts of one of the Union's last great pre–Civil War generals, Winfield "Old Fuss and Feathers" Scott, the hero of the Mexican War. Like Robert E. Lee, Scott was a Virginian, but unlike Lee he remained loyal to the Union; he was well into his seventies by that time and pretty much committed. Scott could barely hoist his three-hundred pounds on gout-riddled feet at war's outbreak, but his mind was sound. Scott was one of the few who foresaw a lengthy war, and his "Anaconda Plan" called for surrounding the South like a snake and choking away its life-giving commerce. The press made wicked fun of strategy plan from the man whose nickname it amended to "Old Fat and Flabby." McClellan and his supporters hounded Scott out of office in 1861, but he lived long enough to see the war through and watch history prove him to be right on just about all accounts.

Both the Union blockade and the Confederate cruisers sought economic destruction; but while the blockade waited for ships to come to it, the South took the battle to wherever Union merchant ships might take them.

Like her sister ships, the *Alabama* was built in British shipyards (Confederate agents could sometimes take advantage of their ties to cotton brokers who had connections in the shipping industry) under an assumed name and civilian dress. These sloops were powered by both steam and sail and were fast and agile. Once they were out of sight of the neutral British, they were fitted with guns and fighting crews and took on new personas. The *Oreto* became the *Florida*, the *Sea King* became the *Shenandoah*, and the *Enrica* became the CSS *Alabama*. The crews were often British, and finding enough of them was often a problem, but upping pay and grog allowances was always helpful in these matters.

The *Alabama* quietly set sail in the summer of 1862 and within two months she was capturing and burning Northern merchant ships. For two years the *Alabama* terrorized Northern commerce, crisscrossing the Atlantic and venturing as far afield as the Indian Ocean and South Pacific. For two years the United Stated Navy tried to track her down without success. She took 2,000 prisoners and captured or destroyed sixty-five ships. Her fellow raiders were not too far behind in their conquests, which not only affected the Northern economy, but also kept Northern warships busy on the high seas, and out of the South's hair near their home ports. Further, the cost of insurance on shipping skyrocketed as a result of the danger presented by the raiders. The U.S. Navy was not amused.

In October 1864, the CSS *Florida* slipped into the neutral port of Bahia, Brazil, with the USS *Wachusett* under command of Napoleon Collins in pursuit. The crew of the *Florida* breathed a sigh of relief and many of them felt it was safe to go ashore, seeing as how the United States ship had no authority in foreign ports. Or so it was assumed. Instead, the scene that played out was almost identical to the movie cliché in which the outlaw believes he is safe from capture because he has crossed the Rio Grande—only to see the U.S. cavalry splash across the river and grab him anyway.

The *Wachusett*, operating under the naval doctrine of "port schmort," steamed right up and opened fire on the *Florida*, which was forced to surrender after token resistance, leaving the *Wachusett* free to tow it back to the states. Brazil filed a formal protest against Collins, who was court-martialed for violating international neutrality and sentenced to be dismissed. The court also ruled that the *Florida* was to be taken back to Brazil where it would in all likelihood be returned to the Confederate Navy.

This is what was supposed to have happened. In point of fact, however, Collins earned a promotion and the *Florida*, worst luck, accidentally sank off the coast of Virginia before it could be sailed back to Brazil. So the *Florida* joined the *Alabama*, which was already at the bottom of the sea, but had arrived there under more violent circumstances.

It had been four months earlier that a cheer had gone up on the decks of the Federal raider-chaser *Kearsarge*, then moored at a port in Holland. News had arrived that the *Alabama* had limped into a French port for repairs, meaning a lengthy nautical hunt was finally over. In two days, the *Kearsarge* was perched like a hawk off the Cherbourg breakwater, and the note from Confederate Captain Semmes to Federal Captain Winslow confirmed that it was game on.

It might not have been the best choice for Semmes, who could have laid up in port for an extended period or snuck out of port under the cover of darkness rather than take on a warship of equal strength *mano y mano*. But even though he had taken down a Union fighting ship, Semmes had been publicly labeled a pirate for his attacks on defenseless merchant ships, which hurt his feelings and struck at his sense of Southern honor. Coward would not be added to his perceived demerits. Besides, Semmes thought he could win.

The *Alabama* took on a hundred tons of coal, which helped barricade her engines from damage and would keep her low in the water, with less surface area for enemy shells to hit. The crew checked the powder and polished the brass. The *Kearsarge* likewise took on fuel, sent valuables to shore and put men to work sharpening cutlasses and pikes. Earlier in the war its sailors had seen to one more task that was to generate much chatter in the days and years to come: They lined the flanks of the ship with chains, and then tacked a veneer of wood over top.

The French, playing the part of referee, shut down communication to the two vessels the day before the fight to prevent any spy-generated dispatches that might offer an unfair advantage. Excitement built, on ship and on shore. At a Saturday night supper in Cherbourg, Southern officers met with French sympathizers to discuss whether the better course would be to sink the Union gunboat or bring her into the Southern fleet. The *Alabama* had many fans as she steamed out of port. Wrote John M. Taylor in *Semmes: Rebel Raider*:

> The clash between the two ships was, among other things, pure theater. It seemed that everyone in France

wanted to watch what would prove to be the last one-on-one duel between wooden ships. Excursion trains brought the curious, and throngs of small craft hovered outside the breakwater. Painter Edouard Manet was among those present; he would later paint the most famous rendition of the battle.

Out in the channel, the men of the *Kearsarge* were starting to think Semmes wasn't going to show. Then in mid-morning, a steamer was sighted emerging from port, and a spyglass confirmed it was the long-sought-after Northern nemesis. The crews of both ships performed one last customary chore: sanding the decks so the sailors wouldn't slip in the blood.

On the Southern ship, Semmes gave a hearty speech. "The name of your ship has become a household word wherever civilization extends [Much cheering]. Shall that name be tarnished by defeat? [Never!] Remember that you are in the English Channel, the theater of so much of the naval glory of our race, [Yes!] and that the eyes of Europe are at this moment are upon you!"

On the Northern ship, Winslow took a steely and quieter calculation. He turned and sailed further into the channel, so the *Alabama* would not be able to quickly duck back into a neutral port should events go poorly for it. The *Alabama* willingly followed. Shortly before 11 a.m., Winslow wheeled the *Kearsarge* around to face her adversary.

At about a mile distant, the *Alabama* began lobbing shells. Aside from some splintered rigging, the *Kearsarge* was undamaged, and the two ships began to circle each other like heavyweights in a boxing ring. The *Alabama* kept up a heavier fire, but most of the shots missed. One that didn't was a shell that screamed into the stern of the Kearsarge and sank into a monolithic piece of timber known as the sternpost, a wooden keystone of sorts that held the aft hull and deck together. The crew held its breath, waiting for an explosion that could have taken down the ship, but the shell was a dud.

After this and a couple of other close calls, the *Kearsarge* began to press the advantage. The hull of the *Alabama* was being pounded, and she was losing men fast. While the firing of the *Alabama* was rapid and wild, wrote historian A. K. Browne, the fire of the *Kearsarge* was "deliberate, precise and almost from the commencement productive of death, destruction and dismay." From shore, all things appeared to be equal. Both ships were putting up a good fight and it was impossible to tell who had the advantage. But for the Confederates, too many things had begun to go wrong.

A perfect shot from the *Kearsarge* knocked out the *Alabama*'s steering. Meanwhile, her own gunners were struggling to get the range. Some blamed inexperience; some blamed stale gunpowder which was going on a year old. Many Confederate shells failed to explode because gunners had failed to properly expose the fuses. And the big guns of the *Kearsarge* were taking a horrific human toll on the Alabama's decks. Wrote Browne:

> *Terrific was the effect of the eleven-inch shell upon the crew of the doomed ship: many were torn asunder by shell direct, or horribly mutilated by splinters. Her decks were covered with blood and the debris of bodies. One gun (after-pivot) had its crew renewed four times, fourteen out of nineteen men being disabled during the action. The carnage around this gun was more frightful than elsewhere;*

so great was the accumulation of blood and fragments of limbs, that a removal was required before the gun could be worked.

Men grabbed shovels and plowed the human remains off the side of the ship and into the sea. In another vivid scene, the ship's physician was treating a wounded soldier when a Union shell blew the patient off the operating table and out from under the doctor's scalpel.

Nothing the Confederates tried worked, from concentrating fire on one particularly troublesome gun to going after the North's officers with sniper fire. And Semmes was noticing something strange. The *Alabama*'s shots that did hit home did not seem to be having much of an effect. He couldn't understand why.

It was over in an hour. The *Alabama* made a break for neutral waters, but was so badly battered it was a hopeless gambit. She went down, stern first, but her officers—rescued by a British ship—avoided capture. The spectators on shore several miles away knew that one ship had gone down, but didn't know which, until the *Kearsarge* came within range of a spyglass. It was not cheered the way the Alabama had been when leaving port that morning.

When Semmes learned after the fact that the Union ship had been protected by chains along its sides, he was ready to fight the battle all over again, taking great offense that such a dishonorable advantage had been secreted away by the *Kearsarge*. Winslow shrugged. The anchor chains had to be stored somewhere, after all. And the wood that shielded them from sight? Just keeping the chains dry. (In truth, scholarship since the battle has indicated the armor played little part in the battle one way or the other.)

The sinking of the *Alabama* and *Florida* didn't end the exploits of the Confederate commerce raiders, and neither did the end of the war. The CSS *Shenandoah* remained at sea, and even after Appomattox had no way of knowing the war was over. She was at the Arctic Circle off Alaska two months after the surrender when an understandably miffed captain of one of her victims produced a San Francisco newspaper detailing Lee's surrender. Choosing not to believe everything they read in the papers, the *Shenandoah*'s crew kept on capturing whaling boats in the Aleutian Islands until a British captain confirmed the veracity of the report in August.

It was fitting, perhaps, that it was one of these renegade raiders that traveled the globe with such daring and aplomb and so often played by their own rules that would wind up firing the last shot of the Civil War—four months after it was over.

CHAPTER 16

Chamberlain's Last Day at the Office

The North's Maj. Gen. Joshua Chamberlain might at the same time be the best-known and least-known officer of the war. In Civil War pop culture and beyond, Chamberlain's undermanned 20th Maine has been well publicized as having been the last wisp of a defense between the Confederate army and Washington, D.C., during the tide-turning Gettysburg campaign. He is a hero in Michael Shaara's novel *Killer Angels*, leading a memorable bayonet charge at a surprised enemy and capturing twice as many men as he had under his own command.

It was indeed a memorable if fleeting moment worthy of its press clippings.

Historian James McPherson wrote that the accolades were certainly deserved, but in a way, unfortunate. Because focusing on Gettysburg "does ironic injustice to Chamberlain. Shaara's novel ends with Lee's retreat at Gettysburg and thus ends most readers' knowledge of Chamberlain. Yet he went on to become one of the most remarkable soldiers of the Civil War—indeed, in all of American history."

For example, few might know that it was Chamberlain, the icon of Gettysburg, who accepted the Confederate's surrender with a gesture that echoed through history. Or that Chamberlain wrote perhaps the most telling Northern chronicle of the war's final days. It can be argued that he put the last nine months of the war into a perspective as no one has been able to replicate; the horrible, eye-averting end of the war might be best seen through Joshua Chamberlain's eyes.

Chamberlain is a fascinating study, but difficult to classify. With Chamberlain, appearances were always deceiving. He sported one of those classic Civil War moustaches that look as if a bat hit him in the face at high speed. His eyebrows hunkered down over a piercing gaze that could be disarming, yet slightly hard to take seriously due to the unfortunate outgrowth on his upper lip. A scholar, politician, and theologian with a keen eye for detail and sentiment, he noticed things others didn't, and with an intellect no other could match. He took his work seriously, yet his writings, like his moustache, betray a wit that—given the overall gravitas of his subject matter—probably seemed a bit funnier than it was.

He could read ancient Greek, but had no schooling in military matters. Thin and bookish, his appearance was deceptive in that he proved to be impossible to kill. He was hit by enemy fire multiple times and had three horses shot out from under him. On three separate occasions, Chamberlain's obituary was printed in Northeastern newspapers; only the last one, in 1914, was accurate.

Joshua Chamberlain is best remembered for his desperate defense of the Union left at the Battle of Gettysburg. But his military career, at that point, was just getting warmed up. (Courtesy National Archives)

Like so many of his fellows, Chamberlain became cannon fodder for Southern guns. Unlike so many of his fellows in Grant's final push to Richmond, he survived.

The year of 1864 was horror for all concerned—not that the other war years were a cakewalk, but the last Federal push south through Virginia was a heartbreaking meat grinder of slaughter in a war that was all over but the shooting. Jefferson Davis and Robert E. Lee would certainly have suspected as much. So would the Confederate soldiers in the field, even if they couldn't admit it (of the ones who could, many simply tossed aside their haversacks and walked away). The only issue left to be settled was the number of men who would die before the formality of surrender occurred. This number would prove to be unthinkable. Thousands of lives were chucked into the furnace of battle in a war that was over a year before it was done.

For the men, it might seem as if fighting had become just a job. Some surely could have been characterized as being institutionalized without the walls. Hell and this freakish campaign were all they knew. At night, if the two sides were camped close enough, the Southerners might begin to sing and the Northerners on the other side of the breastworks would join in, culminating in, as one soldier wrote, a "mighty and thrilling chorus."

In the morning the men who had been singing hymns together the night before would wake up and begin killing each other. Nothing about it made sense. It was death by assembly line. Grant hammered away, correctly enough counting on the North's ever-superior numbers. From May through October of Grant's 1864 Virginia campaign, the Federal's chief field-hospital officer counted 68,540 men who were either killed, wounded, incapacitated by illness (often fatally), or simply disappeared.

"The striking fact is thus established," Joshua Chamberlain observed, "that we had more men killed and wounded in the first six months of Grant's campaign than Lee had at any one period of it in his whole army. This hammering business had been hard on the hammer." So dreadful and unfathomable were the losses, he added, that morning calls went unreported because "the country would not stand it if they knew." For all that, Lee's army was losing even more men as a percentage of his total troops. Marching into Chambersburg on a raiding mission, Southern soldiers had been astonished to see men of fighting age in the North attending to civilian business as usual. In the South, there were no more men; for the South, the war was unsustainable.

It almost wasn't sustainable for Chamberlain either, given his talent for interfering in the path of Southern projectiles. The first time Chamberlain "died" was outside of Petersburg during the siege of 1864. Chamberlain was shot through both hips, a wound that was typically not survivable. As he lay bleeding, Grant promoted him to brigadier general, so he would have the small comfort of dying at that rank. Instead, Chamberlain recovered and went on to lead a division, one step below that of corps commander. Of his wound, he commented, in his Maine way, that he did not have any Virginia blood in him, but Virginia had his.

It needn't necessarily have been that way. Richmond was on every Northern tongue and its capture would have excited headline writers, but it was Petersburg that mattered. It was a center of railroads, supply centers and manufacturing. After absorbing a crippling body blow at Cold Harbor on the outskirts of Richmond in early June (both a personal and a PR disaster for Grant; the South reported eighty-four men killed, the North, 1,844) Grant replaced blunt force with sleight of hand.

It almost worked. His army withdrew from north of Richmond, and in a brash and daring move crossed the James River, moved to the south of lightly defended Petersburg and then—nothing. The officers entrusted to crush Petersburg's meager defenses lost their nerve at a time when speed was critical. By the time they had overcome the cumulative knot in their throat it was too late, and Petersburg's breastworks were now heavily populated with Confederate soldiers. What should have been a quick victory turned into a nine-month siege.

So the war dragged on, and it was in the spring of 1865, not quite a year since his first death, that Chamberlain's next death occurred. It happened on an attack of the Confederate's right flank, as Grant probed for some chink in Petersburg's armor. For the bullet, it was an interesting trip. A Confederate took aim at Chamberlain's chest and fired. But just before the hammer dropped, Chamberlain was having a disagreement with his horse. He buried his heel in the horse's flank, and rather than obey, it rose up on its hind feet. This proved to be good for the officer, but bad for the horse. The bullet entered its neck and passed through before hitting Chamberlain square in front of his heart. But a leather-bound packet of field orders deflected the projectile, and a brass mirror hampered its velocity. It still had enough oomph left to rattle around Chamberlain's rib cage before exiting the back of his coat and striking the aid riding next to him in his sidearm, knocking him from his horse. All in all, it was quite the shot, and whoever fired it never received proper credit.

Chamberlain awoke some time later to the consoling words of Brig. Gen. Charles Griffin, telling him that he was dying. It was an honest mistake. Chamberlain was lying in enough blood to drown a horse, but most of the blood was indeed *from* the horse. Griffin's words of condolences were interrupted by a Rebel yell, and Chamberlain saw his line about to break. With all the dignity he could muster in his condition, he and his wounded horse, Charlemagne, returned to the field where, "I was astonished at the cheers which marked my course. Strangest of all was that when I emerged to the sight of the enemy, they also took up the cheering. I hardly knew what world I was in."

The world got stranger still. Weak from the loss of blood, Charlemagne gave out at an inopportune time that found Chamberlain in advance of his line, where he was soon surrounded by three Confederate soldiers preparing to take him prisoner at bayonet point. Chamberlain's hat was gone. His coat was bloodied and soiled beyond recognition—a policy of deception was worth a shot: "What do you take me for?" he bellowed. "Don't you see these Yanks right onto us?" With a flourish, he led them back toward the federal line. "They did follow me like brave fellows—most of them too far, for they were a long time getting back." In a more somber mood that evening as he surveyed the field fresh with death he mused darkly over the "men made in the image of God, marred by the hand of man . . . Was it God's command we heard, or his forgiveness we must forever implore?"

Eventually, the South was pried out of its position. Lee, his supply lines cut, prepared to move west in a desperate attempt to consolidate his army with what Confederate troops remained under Gen. Joseph Johnston.

Grant relentlessly followed, dogging Lee at every stop, and capturing what little his army had in the way of food and supplies. All but cornered on April 9, Lee had one slim hope. He saw a soft spot in the Federal lines and hit the cavalry of Gen. Phil Sheridan, pushing it back enough to generate some optimism of escape.

At that moment, however, Lee's men looked up to the brow of the hill and were stunned to see a solid line of Chamberlain's infantry and the rest of the 5th Corps—a wall of blue that by all rights had no business being there. Chamberlain, it turned out, had been awakened in the middle of the night and told that Sheridan was in trouble. Shaking sleep from his head, he roused his men and ordered a frantic, forced march in support of the fellow officer. If his men moved fast enough they could slam the door on Lee, and this could finally be it.

No one needed to be told twice. They raced to the source of the Appomattox River in a wide valley that formed something of a natural amphitheater. There, they looked down to see their foe looking back up at them.

The union infantry attacked, but not really. The human spectacle playing in front of them was too heartbreaking, too pathetic, to be a force worthy of actual malice. Chamberlain watched as they struggled in the muddy stream bank and later wrote of what he saw:

> *Around its edges, now trodden to mire, swarms an indescribable crowd; a worn out soldier struggling to the front; demoralized citizen and denizen ... following Lee's army (and) suddenly confronted by terrible Yankees pictured to them as demon-shaped and bent; animals too, of all forms and grades; vehicles of every description and nondescription—public or domestic, four-wheeled or two or one—heading and moving in every direction, a swarming mass of chaotic confusion.*

Chamberlain and his men moved in for the kill, at once excited and reserved. "Had one the heart to strike at beings so helpless" with full fury, the river would have run red with blood, he said. Instead, both sides acted out their parts in this final scene, "wild work that looks like fighting, but not much killing, or even hurting. The disheartened enemy take it easy; our men take them easier."

One of Chamberlain's orderlies, a boy really, asked if he could join the fray. Permission granted, he waved his sword with a flourish and bounded away—returning a short time later with four captured swords clutched to his breast and a proud but mildly puzzled look on his face. He'd have a story to tell the folks back home for sure, but the enemy had surrendered so willingly.

Then, perhaps a mile distant, two riders caught the eyes of Chamberlain and his aides. The horsemen were in between the lines, which was odd. They appeared to be heading toward Chamberlain's command, but dropped down into a hollow and were lost to sight. Then another rider appeared, closer this time. Chamberlain observed the scene, and felt his chest catch as he grasped what was happening:

> [It was] a soldierly young figure, a Confederate staff officer undoubtedly. Now I see the white flag, earnestly borne, and its possible purport sweeps before my inner vision like a wraith of morning mist. He comes steadily on, the mysterious form in gray, my mood so whimsically sensitive that I could even smile at the material of the flag—wondering where in either army was found a towel, and one so white.

The Northern men watched. They saw the rider. Bit by bit the shooting died down and then stopped as the two riders whom Chamberlain had seen earlier emerged to announce Lee's unconditional surrender. One last, unfortunate cannon shot took the life of a nearby Union man after announcement of the truce, one last, cruel symbol of a cruel war.

Having no authority in madders of surrender, Chamberlain sent the heralds up the chain of command, and remained unsure of what to do next. His men had no such reservations. At once, there was a mass push to the front. Everyone wanted to see the end of such a long, arduous journey. They climbed trees, buildings, chimneys, fences, and haystacks. Thousands of hats went airborne, and the men seemed to want to climb the air currents after them. An old Union general, who somehow hadn't gotten the message, bustled up to Chamberlain to ask the meaning of all this deviation from standard discipline. "Only that Lee wants to surrender," was the answer, to which the old man bellowed "Glory to God," and gave Chamberlain a round clamp on the back that "nearly unhorsed us both."

There was relief and some fashion of joy on the Southern side as well, helped by their first taste of a meal in who knew how long. Gen. James Longstreet has approached Union lines "with unwonted moisture on his martial cheek" and said, "Gentlemen, I must speak plainly; we are starving over there." Even though they were short themselves the Union men rustled up some grub and sent it across enemy lines—an act of compassion that was only slightly mitigated by the fact that Sheridan had captured this food from a Southern supply train the night before.

The Southerners wanted to leave their guns in the field and walk away, but Grant felt something a bit more formal was required and the honor was given to Chamberlain to accept the Confederate colors and arms. That morning, Union and Confederate men mingled in one mass of humanity, to talk and to trade mementos for food, tobacco, knives, and shoes. There was deep curiosity to see and speak to the men that they'd been shooting at for the past four years, and before long Appomattox had gained the atmosphere of a country fair, much to the chagrin officers trying to maintain proper decorum.

Chamberlain mused briefly about how he had come to be selected for the honor of accepting the surrender of arms and colors. It was, he believed, because of his studied neutrality. Unlike many generals, he did not hang out with his superiors, he did not try to become anyone's pet, he did not spend a lot of time talking to the press in hope of a positive write-up and he did not play favorites or belittle other officers behind their backs. For this, Grant perhaps had faith that Chamberlain guaranteed him the one attribute that, sadly, a number of officers lacked: dignity.

Grant was certainly mindful of the moment and contemplative of the future when the nation would again stand as one. It was early April. Planting time was passing by. He permitted Southerners to keep their horses and anything else that might help them get in a crop, and offered to help the soldiers find a quick ride home.

The morning of April 12 was cold and gray and bittersweet. Once proud units on both sides had been cut to pieces and reformed, joined up with the tattered remnants of other units that had been similarly decimated. Brigades now were patchwork affairs. So many men were gone. The Federals watched as the soldiers on the opposite stream bank carefully folded their tents for the last time and slowly, dispiritedly broke camp. Chamberlain did not see Confederates; he saw Americans.

And now they move . . . Before us in proud humiliation
stood the embodiment of manhood: men whom neither

toils nor sufferings, nor the fact of death, nor disaster, nor hopelessness could bend from their resolve; standing before us now, thin, worn and famished, but erect, and with eyes looking level into ours, walking memories that bound us together as no other bond—was not such manhood to be welcomed back into a Union so tested and assured?

Chamberlain had no authority to do what he was about to do. It would shower criticism upon his head, sure, but it didn't matter to him, and he made no apology for it. Confederate Lt. Gen. John Gordon led the first Southern column toward the Union ranks, where his men were to turn in their rifles and tattered, blood-spattered battle flags. The general's head was slumped as he rode his horse dully past the Federal ranks.

Instead of watching passively and perhaps basking in the South's humiliation as so many might have done, Chamberlain instead stood at attention and snapped the order for his men to "carry arms," the universal salute of honor. The gallant men of the North were paying their respects to the gallant men of the South. Gordon started in his saddle, and for a split second failed to grasp the meaning of what had just taken place.

[He] catches the sound of shifting arms, looks up and, taking the meaning, wheels superbly, making with himself and his horse one uplifted figure, with profound salutation as he drops the point of the sword to the boot toe; then, facing to his own command, gives word for his successive brigades to pass us with the same position of the manual— honor answering honor.

The Confederates dressed their lines as best they could, exausted and half-starved as they were. Sometimes decorum held, sometimes not as the men gave up their flags, clutching them one last time to their breasts or adding the stain of tears to the battered fabric. The Union troops watched in silence— no catcalls, no taunts. Not even a cheer or outward sign of bravado.

"What visions thronged as we looked into each other's eyes!" Chamberlain wrote. They recognized the men they had seen across the smoky lines of the Cornfield and Bloody Lane at Antietam; Jackson's men who crushed the Union right at Chancellorsville; the Georgia boys who held the stone wall at Fredericksburg; and the few survivors of Quaker Road, their only shortcoming being "too fierce for their own good." A. P. Hill's old corps passed, but A. P. Hill was gone. The new faces in some brigades were unfamiliar—all those old, recognizable faces that once populated their ranks were gone too.

The men of both sides watched each other, lost in their own personal reflections. Arms were stacked, and colors grudgingly surrendered. The proud Confederate army turned to go, in the shadow of a fluttering red, white, and blue flag that was once again theirs.

Selected Bibliography

Books

Ayers, Edward L. *In the Presence of Mine Enemies*. New York: W.W. Norton & Company, 2003.

Blackwell, Sarah Ellen. *A Military Genius: Life of Anna Ella Carroll of Maryland*. Washington, D.C.: Judd & Detweiler; 1891.

Brown, A. K. *The Story of the Kearsarge and Alabama*. San Francisco: Henry Payot & Co., 1868.

Carman, Ezra, ed., Thomas G. Clemens. *The Maryland Campaign of September 1862, Vol. 1, South Mountain*. New York: Savas Beatie, 2010.

Carroll, Anna Ella. *The Relation of The National Government to the Revolted States Defined*. Pamphlet available through the Library of Congress at http://memory.loc.gov/ammem/index .html

Castel, Albert E. *Decision in the West: The Atlanta Campaign of 1864*. Lawrence: University Press of Kansas, 1992.

Chamberlain, Joshua. *The Passing of the Armies*. New York: Bantam Books, 1993.

Davis, Burke. *Jeb Stuart: The Last Cavalier*. New York: Rinehart & Company, Inc., 1957.

De Peyster, John Watts. *Personal and Military History of Philip Kearny, Major-General United States Volunteers*. New York: Palmer & Co., 1870.

Donaldson, Alfred L. *History of the Adirondacks*. Fleischmanns, N.Y.: Purple Mountain Press, 1921.

Doubleday, Abner. *Reminiscences of Forts Sumter and Moultrie*. New York: Harper & Brothers, 1876.

Edge, Frederick Milnes. *The Alabama and the Kearsarge*. Philadelphia: King & Baird, 1868.

Edmonds, S. Emma. *Nurse and Spy in the Union Army: The Adventures and Experiences of a Woman in Hospitals, Camps and Battle-Fields*. Hartford, Conn.: W.S. Williams & Co., 1865.

Eggleston, George Cary. *A Rebel's Recollections*. New York: Hurd and Houghton, 1875.

Ferguson, Niall. *The Ascent of Money: A Financial History of the World*. New York: The Penguin Press, 2008.

Gage, Matilda Joslyn. *Who Planned the Tennessee Campaign of 1862?* Pamphlet reproduced at http://www.archive.org /stream/whoplannedthetenn00gagerich#page/n1/mode/2up

Goodwin, Doris Kearns. *Team of Rivals: The Political Genius of Abraham Lincoln*. New York: Simon & Schuster, 2005.

Greenbie, Sydney and Marjorie Latta Barstow Greenbie. *Anna Ella Carroll and Abraham Lincoln*. Tampa: University of Tampa Press in cooperation with Falmouth Publishing Company, 1952.

Groom, Winston. *Shrouds of Glory*. New York: Grove Press, 1995.

Hansen, Harry. *The Civil War*. New York: Signet Classics, 2002.

Hessler, James A. *Sickles at Gettysburg*. New York: Savas Beatie, 2009.

Johnson, Robert Underwood and Clarence Clough Buel, (ed.). *Battles and Leaders of the Civil War*. New York: The Century Co., 1887–88. Four-volume set available online from Ohio State online library, http://ehistory.osu.edu/osu/books/battles/index.cfm

Keneally, Thomas. *American Scoundrel: The Life of the Notorious Civil War General Dan Sickles*. New York: Nan A. Talese /Doubleday, 2002.

McClellan, George B., ed., and Frank Moore. *The Rebellion Record: Gen. McClellan's Report*. New York: Putnam, 1864.

McPherson, James M. *Battle Cry of Freedom: The Civil War Era*. New York: Oxford University Press, 1988.

Nelson, John H. *Bombard and be Damned: The Effects of Jackson's Valley Campaign on Hancock, Maryland and Fulton County, Pennsylvania.* McConnellsburg, PA: Keystone Printing, 1997.

Oates, Stephen B. *To Purge This Land With Blood: A Biography of John Brown.* Amherst: University of Massachusetts Press, 1984.

Pittenger, Lt. William. *Daring and Suffering: A History of the Great American Railroad Adventure.* Philadelphia: J. W. Daughaday, 1863.

Schneck, Benjamin Shroder. *The Burning of Chambersburg, Pennsylvania.* Philadelphia: Lindsay & Blakiston, 1864.

Stanley, Henry M. (ed. Dorothy Stanley). *The Autobiography of Henry M. Stanley.* New York: Houghton Mifflin, 1909.

Thomas, Emory M. *Bold Dragoon: The Life of J.E.B. Stuart.* New York: Random House, 1988.

Twain, Mark. *Autobiography of Mark Twain.* Berkeley: University of California Press, 2010.

Wainwright, Charles S., ed., and Allan Nevins. *A Diary of Battle: The Personal Journals of Colonel Charles S. Wainwright, 1861-1865.* New York: Harcourt, Brace & World, 1962.

Werstein, Irving. *Kearny the Magnificent.* New York: The John Day Co., 1962.

Wiley, Bell Irvin. *The Life of Billy Yank*. Baton Rouge: Louisiana State University Press, 1952.

Wiley, Bell Irvin. *The Life of Johnny Reb*. Baton Rouge: University of Louisiana State Press, 1943.

Magazine and Newspaper Articles

Robbins, Peggy. "The Confederacy's Bomb Brothers." *Civil War Times*, Leesburg, Va., 1997, reprinted in *The Journal of Mine Action*, April 2002, http://maic.jmu.edu/journal/6.1/notes/robbins/robbins.htm

Stump, Brice. "A Name Long Lost: Anna Ella Carroll." *Delmarva Times*, Sept. 26, 2010; Lifestyle.

The (Hagerstown, Md) Herald of Freedom and Torch Light. Vol. 24, No. 10; Sept. 24, 1862. Other editions are searchable at the Historic Newspaper Indexing Project, http://www.washcolibrary.org/localhistory/newsindex.asp

New York Times Archives, http://www.nytimes.com/ref/membercenter/nytarchive.html

Websites

Abraham Lincoln and the Border States; Gienapp, William E.; www.historycooperative.org/journals/jala/13/gienapp.html

Antietam on the Web http://antietam.aotw.org/exhibit.php?exhibit_id=3

Carter, Rosalie; Capt. Tod Carter of the Confederate States Army; 1978; http://www.tennessee-scv.org/Camp854/todbio.htm

ExplorePAhistory.com. "Burning of Chambersburg." http://explorepahistory.com/hmarker.php?markerId=730

Hunter, R.M.T. "Origin of the Late War: Southern Historical Society Papers." William Jones, ed.; http://www.perseus.tufts.edu/hopper/text?doc=Perseus%3atext%3a2001.05.0001

New York Military Affairs Symposium. "The Tennessee River Campaign." http://bobrowen.com/nymas/tennesseeriver.html

Office of Coast Survey; Civil War Maps and Charts. http://www.nauticalcharts.noaa.gov/staff/news/headline-civilwar-charts.html

Perseus Digital Library; http://www.perseus.tufts.edu/hopper/searchresults?q=civil+war

Shotgun's Home of the American Civil War; http://www.civilwarhome.com/

Tennessee Division Document Archive; http://www.tennessee-scv.org/archive.htm

"U.S. History; Strengths and Weaknesses, North vs. South." http://www.ushistory.org/us/33b.asp

Valley of the Shadow Project. http://valley.lib.virginia.edu/

Washington County Free Library Historic Newspaper Indexing Project. "The Raid." http://www.washcolibrary.org/localhistory/articles.asp?aID=1